Then Comes the End

by Mike Willis

Truth Publications / CEIbooks
220 S. Marion St., Athens, AL 35611
855.492.6657 | sales@ceibooks.com

ISBN 10: 1-58427-005-5

ISBN 13: 978-158427-005-8

Second Printing 2007

Third Printing 2011

Fourth Printing 2016

Truth Publications / CEIbooks

220 S. Marion St., Athens, AL 35611

855.492.6657 | sales@ceibooks.com

Table of Contents

Lesson 1

Physical Death

Death is a part of human existence. Without death, the earth would long ago have been overpopulated and human suffering have increased. But what is death? Webster's dictionary definition of "death" is "the act of dying; permanent cessation of life in a person, animal, or plant, in which all vital functions cease permanently." To have a biblical understanding of death, one must understand what man is and why death came.

Man is composed of "body, soul, and spirit" (1 Thess. 5:23). The body refers to the flesh and bones of which man is made; the soul is used in this verse to refer to the life that an animate object has in contrast to an inanimate object (contrast a rock and a dog);[1] the spirit refers to that immortal part of man that is made in the image of God (Gen. 1:26). In creation, God made man from the dust of the earth (his body), breathed into his nostrils the breath of life (his soul), and made him in his own image (his spirit) (see Gen. 1:26; 2:7). Man is, therefore, composed of body, soul, and spirit.

James said "the body without the spirit is dead" (James 2:26). So long as the body and spirit are together, man is alive. When the spirit leaves the body, death occurs. Thayer defines *thanatos* as follows: "**1.** prop. *the death of the body*, i.e. *that separation* (whether natural or violent) *of the soul from the body by which the life on earth is ended* " (282). Death is that time when the immortal spirit departs from the fleshly body, leaving it without life.

[1] The Greek word *psuche* is sometimes used to refer to the spirit of man. The context of each verse must be studied to determine whether *psuche* refers to the immortal spirit or is used in some other way. See Thayer (677) for a study of the word's different uses.

The Origin of Death

The Old Testament records how death entered the world. When God created man, he placed him in the Garden of Eden to tend and care for the Garden (Gen. 2:15). He gave him this commandment, "Of every tree of the garden thou mayest freely eat: but of the tree of the knowledge of good and evil, thou shalt not eat of it: for in the day that thou eatest thereof thou shalt surely die" (Gen 2:16-17). The Devil used this commandment to murder the entire human race (John 8:44). He deceived Eve and she in turn persuaded Adam

to sin. As a consequence of this sin, man was separated from the tree of life and death passed upon all men (Gen. 3:19, 22-23; Rom. 5:12). Because of Adam's sin, death comes to all men (1 Cor. 15:21).

The Bible records the first death when Cain killed Abel (Gen. 4:8). The genealogies of Genesis 5 have this sad refrain "and he died" (5:5, 8, 11, 14, 17, 20, 27). Death is the common experience of the human race. "And as it is appointed unto men once to die, but after this the judgment" (Heb. 9:27).

Death comes to the physical body because of Adam's sin (Rom. 8:10-11). Even those who have not sinned in the likeness of Adam's transgression face physical death (Rom. 5:14). Babies die in infancy, even though they have never personally committed sin, as a consequence of physical death coming upon all men because of Adam's sin.

In some respects death is a blessing. As we previously mentioned, were death not present, the world would long ago have become over populated and, with so many vying for the necessities of life, war, theft, and other forms of anarchy would surely be multiplied. In the second century, Irenaeus wrote about death saying,

> Wherefore He (God) drove him out of Paradise, and removed him far from the tree of life, not because He envied the tree of life, as some venture to assert, but because He pitied him, [and did not desire] that he should continue a sinner for ever, nor that the sin which surrounded him should be immortal, and evil interminable and irremedial. But He set a bound to his [state of] sin, by imposing death, and thus causing sin to cease, putting an end to it by the dissolution of the flesh, which should take place in the earth, so that man, ceasing at length to live to sin, and dying to it, might begin to live to God (*Against Heresies*, xxiii.6).

In texts that address the issue of suffering death for Christ, some authors viewed the day of one's martyrdom as his spiritual birthday. This is first seen in *The Martyrdom of Saint Polycarp* in which the author writes, "There the Lord will permit us as far as possible, to assemble in rapturous joy and celebrate his (Polycarp's) martyrdom—his birthday—both in order to commemorate the heroes that have gone before, and to train and prepare heroes yet to come" (18). The concept is continued in later Christian authors, such as Ignatius who described the process of dying as "birth pangs" (see footnote 51 of above quote from *The Martyrdom*).

Causes of Death
- **Disease**
- **Accident**
- **Murder**
- **Suicide**
- **Decay**

Under Death's Power

The writer of Hebrews explained that Jesus had to become a man to deliver those who are under the power of death. He wrote, "Forasmuch then as the children are partakers of flesh and blood, he also himself likewise took part of the same; that through death he might destroy him that had the power of death, that is, the devil; and deliver them who through fear of death were all their lifetime subject to bondage" (Heb. 2:14-15). The devil holds men in his power requiring them

Shall We Pull the Plug?

From time to time, family members are faced with the problem of deciding when to end the treatment of one whose life is being sustained by mechanical means. The doctors report that brain activity has ceased. The patient is being kept alive by a respirator and other medical devices (kidney dialysis, for example). After heroic efforts have been made to save the patient's life, the patient is not improving and the valiant attempts of the medical community are only prolonging the death process. What should we do?

The issue is sometimes described as the issue of euthanasia. Medical ethics distinguishes between two kinds of euthanasia: (a) active euthanasia in which the doctors give the patient medication to end one's life; (b) passive euthanasia in which some things which could be done to sustain life are withheld (insertion of feeding tubes, putting the patient on oxygen, etc.). As doctors wrestled with the issue, the solution at which they arrived is that which is followed by the hospice treatment. Doctors recognize that nothing more can be done for the patient. The patient is not ever going to be restored to health and death is coming. In such situations, the doctors and nurses' role is to make the patient as comfortable as possible as they go through the process of dying. In such cases, a highly addictive drug, such as morphine, is administered in amounts that would normally would lead to addiction were the patient to continue to live, in order to prevent the patient from enduring horrible pain in the process of dying.

The medical community cannot provide eternal physical life, despite all of their medical advances. One must accept, whether or not he wishes to, that death is a part of the process of life.

to face physical death. We are under the "power of death," live under the "fear of death," and are "subject to bondage." For this reason, Jesus died on the cross of Calvary to redeem us from the bondage of death. He who conquered death by the resurrection will raise our dead bodies at his second coming.

Sickness and Death

Inasmuch as men live in a world under God's sentence of physical death, one can expect that accidents and sickness will come to man. On one occasion, some Jews spoke to Jesus about the tragedies of life.

> There were present at that season some that told him of the Galilaeans, whose blood Pilate had mingled with their sacrifices. And Jesus answering said unto them, Suppose ye that these Galilaeans were sinners above all the Galilaeans, because they suffered such things? I tell you, Nay: but, except ye repent, ye shall all likewise perish. Or those eighteen, upon whom the tower in Siloam fell, and slew them, think ye that they were sinners above all men that dwelt in Jerusalem? I tell you, Nay: but, except ye repent, ye shall all likewise perish (Luke 13:1-5).

These tragedies were not proof that men were greater sinners than others (as if physical suffering was related to personal offenses). Sometimes men who face tragedies in their lives reason that somehow those tragedies are the result of God punishing their sinful conduct. Jesus plainly tells them that is not true.

Here are some explanations about death which men offer. To explain the death of a baby, one may say, "God needed another angel, so he took my child." To explain the death of a righteous person, someone may say, "God is punishing those who are left behind." Another may say, "Satan directly intervened in the affairs of men

Set Your House in Order

2 Kings 20:1 says, "In those days was Hezekiah sick unto death. And the prophet Isaiah the son of Amoz came to him, and said unto him, Thus saith the Lord, Set thine house in order; for thou shalt die, and not live" (2 Kings 20:1). Sometimes we make a spiritual application of this Old Testament text, and certainly one needs to make preparation spiritually for the day of his death, but there are also some temporal preparations one needs to make for the day of his death. Think about these:

Younger couples. The likelihood of death striking a younger couple is less than for older couples, but it sometimes does happen. Would your house be set in order for that eventuality? Think about some of the responsibilities that one might have:

- Would your wife be financially prepared to provide for the children?
- Do you have enough insurance to pay for medical bills, funeral expenses, and sustain her through a transition to living without you being present?
- Should the wife die, does the husband have the financial means to provide for the children (medical bills, burial expenses, increased expenses of hiring child care while he works, etc.).

Older couples. Death is certain to be an unwanted visitor in the home of those who are older. Though the medical community has made great advancements in overcoming life-threatening illnesses, death is still certain and it can only be postponed, not averted. Here are some things you need to think about:

- Purchasing your grave plot.
- Pre-paying your funeral expenses.
- Acquainting your mate with the necessary papers he/she will need at your passing.
- Planning your funeral (who do you want to preach it, what songs do you want sung, who should be your pallbearers, etc.).

The more of these things you prepare for ahead of time, the fewer things the surviving spouse and/or children will have to fret over during their period of grief.

Have you given any thought to setting your house in order?

to cause someone to die." In a world under the judgment of death, accidents, sickness and death are ordinary occurrences. We should not believe that God is personally angry at a person because of an unusual death. Even God's own Son suffered a tragic death.

Death Is Certain

If the world tarries, men will continue to die and, therefore, my own death is certain to occur. Consider these passages that speak of the certainty of death:

> All flesh shall perish together, and man shall turn again unto dust (Job 34:15).
>
> There is no man that hath power over the spirit to retain the spirit; neither hath he power in the day of death: and there is no discharge in that war; neither shall wickedness deliver those that are given to it (Eccl. 8:8).
>
> For the living know that they shall die: but the dead know not any thing, neither have they any more a reward; for the memory of them is forgotten (Eccl. 9:5).
>
> And as it is appointed unto men once to die, but after this the judgment (Heb 9:27).

Jesus Changed Our View of Death

Jesus' resurrection was the victory over death (Rom. 6:9) and the assurance of his certain victory over death in the resurrection at the second coming (1 Cor. 15:20-26). He brought life and immortality to light through the gospel (2 Tim. 1:10). From the following passages, consider to what death is compared:

- The departing of the soul (Jas. 2:26; Gen. 25:8; 35:18; Luke 23:46; Acts 7:59).
- A departure (2 Tim. 4:6; Phil. 1:23; Ps. 90:10).
- A putting off of this tabernacle (2 Pet. 1:13-14; 2 Cor. 5:1, 4, 6-8).
- A sleep (Job 7:21; John 11:20-24).
- Rest (Rev. 14:13).
- A sting (1 Cor. 15:56).

Figurative Uses of Death

Death is used to describe two other separations besides the separation of the body from the spirit:

1. Separation From God: Spiritual Death. One who is separated from God by his sin is said to be dead in his trespasses and sins (Eph. 2:1, 5). In this sense, Adam died in the day that he ate of the forbidden fruit (Gen. 2:17), even though he lived to be 930 years old.

2. Hell: The Second Death. The everlasting separation from God in Hell is described as the "second death" (Rev. 2:11; 20:4, 14; 21:8).

NOTES

Questions

1. Give a dictionary definition of death. ______________________________
2. How are death and sin related (Gen. 2:16-17)? ______________________________
3. In what sense is death a punishment for sin? ______________________________
4. In what sense is the Devil said to be a murderer (John 8:44)? ______________________________
5. What is the curse that sin brought to the human race (Gen. 3:19-23)? ______________________________
6. What part did separation from the tree of life play in the cause of death? ______________________________
7. In what sense is death an act of God's mercy? ______________________________
8. Who was the first man to die? ______________________________
9. How many times does "and he died" appear in Genesis 5? What is the point of this being repeated so many times? ______________________________
10. How is Adam the cause of death (Rom. 5:12)? ______________________________
11. In what sense is the body dead because of sin (Rom. 8:10-11)? ______________________________

12. In what sense did all men die because of one man (1 Cor. 15:21)? ________

____

13. Who has the "power of death" (Heb. 2:14-15)? ________

14. In what sense does man live in the "fear of death" (Heb. 2:14-15)? ________

____

15. In what sense is man in "bondage" to death (Heb. 2:14-15)? ________

____

16. How did Jesus relate accidents to personal sin (Luke 13:1-5)? ________

____

17. How might sickness and accidents be used by God to remind us to "repent or perish"? ________

____

18. Analyze the following statements frequently made about death and compare them with what the Bible teaches about death.

    a. "God needed another angel, so he took my child." ________

    ____

    b. "God is punishing those who are left behind." ________

    ____

    c. "Satan directly intervened in the affairs of men to cause death." ________

    ____

19. What do the following passages reveal about the certainty of death?

    a. Eccl. 8:8. ________

    b. Eccl. 9:5. ________

    c. Heb. 9:27. ________

    d. Job 34:15. ________

20. To what do the Scriptures compare death in the following passages:

    a. James 2:26; Gen. 25:8; 35:18; Luke 23:46; Acts 7:59. ________

    b. 2 Tim. 4:6; Phil. 1:23; Ps. 90:10. ________

    c. 2 Pet. 1:13-14; 2 Cor. 5:1, 4, 6-8. ________

    d. Job 7:21; John 11:20-24. ________

e. Rev. 14:13. ______________________________

f. 1 Cor. 15:56. ______________________________

21. The Scriptures depict Hell as the "second death" (Rev. 2:11; 20:6, 14; 21:8). Why is it called the "second death"? ______________________________

____

22. Why is one said to be "dead" in sin (Eph. 2:1, 5)? ______________________________

____

Lesson 2

The Immortality of the Soul

Some religious groups, such as the Jehovah's Witnesses, deny that man has an immortal soul that survives the death of the body. The Seventh Day Adventists believe that the soul "sleeps" or is in a state of unconscious existence between death and the resurrection. This lesson is designed to show that man has a spirit made in the image of God which has conscious existence between death and the bodily resurrection at the end of time.

The Scriptures teach that man is composed of body, soul, and spirit (1 Thess. 5:23). Sometimes, we say that man is made up of body and soul (Matt. 10:28), meaning by "soul" that part of man which is made in the image of God and equivalent to the word "spirit" in 1 Thessalonians 5:23. We need to understand what the Scriptures teach about the word "soul." The word *psuchē* is used in a number of ways in the Scriptures. The chart illustrates the various uses of the word.

The Uses of the Word "Soul"

Animal Life	Human Life	Persons	Immortal Part of Man
Rev. 16:3 Num. 31:28	Matt. 2:20 Luke 12:22 Acts 20:10 Rev. 8:9; 12:11 Rom. 16:4 Phil. 2:30 1 Thess. 5:23 Heb. 4:12	Gen. 17:14; 46:18 Acts 2:41, 43 1 Pet. 3:20 Rom. 13:1	Matt. 10:28 Acts 2:27 Rev. 6:9; 20:4 James 5:20

The Uses of the Word Soul (*Psuchē*)

Sometimes one is surprised to learn what he already knows. That may be true in this case. One must recognize that the same word is sometimes used with widely different meanings. For example, *Webster's Dictionary* says that the English word "heart" can mean each of the following:

- Blood pump.
- Part of body (chest) that contains the heart
- Seat of the emotions
- Inner part of anything
- The chief part
- A person: "He is a valiant heart" (person).
- That which has the shape of a heart
- A suit of playing cards

Just as we understand that the English word "heart" has several different meanings, one should recognize that the Hebrew (*nephesh*) and the Greek words (*psuchē*) for "soul" have different uses. Here are some of the ways in which these words are used.

1. Animal life. In Revelation 16:3 and Numbers 31:28 (in the LXX), the word "soul" is used to refer to living creatures in distinction from inanimate objects. In Revelation 16:3, "every living soul (*psuchē*)" in the KJV is translated "every living thing" in the NRSV and NIV.

2. Human life. In a number of passages, *psuchē* refers to human life.

> Saying, Arise, and take the young child and his mother, and go into the land of Israel: for they are dead which sought the young child's life (*psuchē*) (Matt. 2:20).

> And he said unto his disciples, Therefore I say unto you, Take no thought for your life (*psuchē*), what ye shall eat; neither for the body, what ye shall put on (Luke 12:22).

> And Paul went down, and fell on him, and embracing him said, Trouble not yourselves; for his life (*psuchē*) is in him (Acts 20:10).

> And they overcame him by the blood of the Lamb, and by the word of their testimony; and they loved not their lives (*psuchē*) unto the death (Rev. 12:11).

3. Persons. The word *psuchē* is sometimes used a synonym for a person. The following uses of *psuchē*, some taken from the LXX version of the Old Testament and some from the New Testament, demonstrate this use:

> And the uncircumcised man child whose flesh of his foreskin is not circumcised, that soul (*psuchē*) shall be cut off from his people; he hath broken my covenant (Gen. 17:14).

> These are the sons of Zilpah, whom Laban gave to Leah his daughter, and these she bare unto Jacob, even sixteen souls (*psuchē*) (Gen. 46:18).

> Then they that gladly received his word were baptized: and the same day there were added unto them about three thousand souls (*psuchē*) (Acts 2:41).

> And fear came upon every soul (*psuchē*): and many wonders and signs were done by the apostles (Acts 2:43).

> Let every soul (*psuchē*) be subject unto the higher powers. For there is no power but of God: the powers that be are ordained of God (Rom. 13:1).

> Which sometime were disobedient, when once the longsuffering of God waited in the days of Noah, while the ark was a preparing, wherein few, that is, eight souls (*psuchē*) were saved by water (1 Pet. 3:20).

4. The immortal part of man. These Bible verses demonstrate that the word *psuchē* is used to refer to that part of man that does not cease to exist when death comes to the body:

> And fear not them which kill the body, but are not able to kill the soul (*psuchē*): but rather fear him which is able to destroy both soul and body in hell (Matt. 10:28).

> Because thou wilt not leave my soul in hell, neither wilt thou suffer thine Holy One to see corruption (Acts 2:27).

> Let him know, that he which converteth the sinner from the error of his way shall save a soul (*psuchē*) from death, and shall hide a multitude of sins (Jas. 5:20)

> And when he had opened the fifth seal, I saw under the altar the souls (*psuchē*) of them that were slain for the word of God, and for the testimony which they held (Rev. 6:9).

> And I saw thrones, and they sat upon them, and judgment was given unto them: and I saw the souls (*psuchē*) of them that were beheaded for the witness of Jesus, and for the word of God, and which had not worshipped the beast, neither his image, neither had received his mark upon their foreheads, or in their hands; and they lived and reigned with Christ a thousand years (Rev. 20:4).

In each of these uses of the word, *psuchē* is used to describe a part of man that survives in conscious existence the death of the physical body.

Sometimes a Christian is surprised when Jehovah's Witnesses say that a "soul" can die. In uses 1-3, that would be true. However, what the Jehovah's Witnesses refuse to admit is that the word "soul" is also used, as in number 4, to describe that part of man that survives the death of the body.

Evidences That Man's Soul Is Immortal

1. The soul is that part of man which is made in the image of God. The creation account tells us that man is made in the image of God (Gen. 1:26). Since God is a spirit and does not have flesh and blood, the only part of man that can be made in God's image is his spirit or soul. For that reason, the Scriptures teach that God is the

NOTES

Father of man's spirit (Heb. 12:9).

2. At death the soul departs from the body but continues to live. Notice the Scripture's picture of death:

> And it came to pass, *as her soul was in departing*, (for she died) that she called his name Benoni: but his father called him Benjamin (Gen. 35:18).
>
> And the Lord heard the voice of Elijah; and *the soul of the child came into him again*, and he revived (1 Kings 17:22).
>
> For as *the body without the spirit is dead*, so faith without works is dead also (James 2:26).

"For we know that if our earthly house of this tabernacle were dissolved, we have a building of God, an house not made with hands, eternal in the heavens. For in this we groan, earnestly desiring to be clothed upon with our house which is from heaven: If so be that being clothed we shall not be found naked. For we that are in this tabernacle do groan, being burdened: not for that we would be unclothed, but clothed upon, that mortality might be swallowed up of life. (2 Cor. 5:1-4) .

Other Passages Showing That Man's Life Continues Following Death

1. 2 Corinthians 4:16-18. *"For* which cause we faint not; but though our outward man perish, yet the inward man is renewed day by day. For our light affliction, which is but for a moment, worketh for us a far more exceeding and eternal weight of glory; while we look not at the things which are seen, but at the things which are not seen: for the things which are seen are temporal; but the things which are not seen are eternal." This passages speaks of man's "outward" and "inward" part. The inward man is "renewed day by day" and will receive an "eternal" weight of glory.

2. 2 Corinthians 5:1-10. The theme of the preceding chapter is continued in this text which speaks of man's earthly house in which he tabernacles (the body) is dissolved, but he is clothed with "an house not made with hands, eternal in the heavens" (5:1). When death occurs, man does not cease to exist, but is in that condition of being "absent from the body" and "present with the Lord" (5:8).

3. Philippians 1:21-23. Paul said, "For to me to live is Christ, and to die is gain. But if I live in the flesh, this is the fruit of my labour: yet what I shall choose I wot not. For I am in a strait betwixt two, having a desire to depart, and to be with Christ; which is far better." Notice that at death, Paul would depart to be with Christ.

4. 1 Peter 3:18-19. Peter wrote, "For Christ also hath once suffered for sins, the just for the unjust, that he might bring us to God, being put to death in the flesh, but quickened by the Spirit: by which also he went and preached unto the spirits in prison." The wicked are described as "spirits in prison." Their existence continued after the death of this body.

5. 2 Peter 2:4-9. In this text, Peter assures us that God can preserve the righteous from destruction and keep the wicked in reserve for their eternal punishment.

6. Luke 23:43. Jesus said to the penitent thief on the cross, "To day shalt thou be with me in paradise" (Luke 23:43).

NOTES

7. Matthew 17:1-9. The Transfiguration of Jesus occurred when Elijah and Moses appeared with him on the mountain. These had been dead for years and yet they were existing and living.

8. Matthew 22:23-33. In Jesus' response to the Sadducees' question about the resurrection, he stated that God is not the God of the dead, but of the living, implying that those who are dead are still living.

Conclusion

The Bible teaches that man's spirit continues to exist after the death of the body. It is conscious and aware of the things that occur on earth (see Luke 16:19-31; Heb. 12:1-2). Death is not the end of man's existence.

NOTES

Questions

1. What does the Bible mean when it refers to animals having a soul (Rev. 16:3; Num. 31:28)? ______

2. Notice the translation of *psuchē* by the word "life" (Matt. 2:20; Luke 12:22). What does the word mean in that context? ______

3. In what sense is the word used in Genesis 17:14; 46:18; 1 Peter 3:20? ______

4. In what sense is the word used in Matthew 10:28; Revelation 6:9; 20:4? ______

5. What do the passages in the "immortal soul of man" section show about the soul's existence after death? ______

6. God is a immortal Spirit and we are his offspring (Acts 17:28; Heb. 12:9). In what sense is man made in God's image? ______

7. What occurs at death (Jas. 2:26; Gen. 35:18; 1 Kings 17:22)? ______

8. Explain what the following passages teach about the soul of man after death:
   a. 2 Corinthians 4:16-18. ______
   b. 2 Corinthians 5:1-10. ______
   c. Philippians 1:21, 23. ______
   d. 1 Peter 3:18-19. ______
   e. 2 Peter 2:4. ______
   f. Luke 23:43. ______

9. What does the Transfiguration show about the dead (Matt. 17:1-9)? ______

10. How did Jesus react to the Sadducees' doctrine of the dead (Matt. 22:23-33)? ______

11. What did these Old Testament saints expect after their deaths?
    a. Job 19:23-27? ______
    b. Psalm 16:9-11? ______
    c. Psalm 17:15? ______

d. Psalm 49:15? ______

e. Psalm 73:24? ______

d. Isaiah 26:19? ______

12. How are the following ideas used as funerals to substitute for the doctrine of the immortality of the soul and the resurrection of the dead?

    a. Immortality of commemoration ("he will be forever remembered by us"): ______

    ______

    b. Immortality of influence ("his influence will live forever through those whose lives he affected"):

    ______

    ______

Lesson 3

Hades: The Intermediate State

We have previously shown that the soul of man survives the death of the body. The departed spirit of man maintains conscious existence after departing this life. Notice the following passages that indicate this:

> Then shall the dust return to the earth as it was: and the spirit shall return unto God who gave it (Eccl. 12:7).
>
> And fear not them which kill the body, but are not able to kill the soul: but rather fear him which is able to destroy both soul and body in hell (Matt. 10:28).
>
> And when he had opened the fifth seal, I saw under the altar the souls of them that were slain for the word of God, and for the testimony which they held: and they cried with a loud voice, saying, How long, O Lord, holy and true, dost thou not judge and avenge our blood on them that dwell on the earth? (Rev. 6:9-10).
>
> And I saw thrones, and they sat upon them, and judgment was given unto them: and I saw the souls of them that were beheaded for the witness of Jesus, and for the word of God, and which had not worshipped the beast, neither his image, neither had received his mark upon their foreheads, or in their hands; and they lived and reigned with Christ a thousand years (Rev. 20:4).

Sheol: The Place of the Departed Spirits in the Old Testament

The King James Version translates the Hebrew word *sheol* by the word "hell," but this translation is not accurate. We will reserve the word "hell" to translate the Greek word *gehenna*. *Sheol* is defined as follows: "underworld ... whither men descend at death" (Brown, Driver, and Briggs, *Hebrew and English Lexicon of the Old Testament* 982). *Sheol* is the place of the dead (Ps. 55:15; Prov. 5:5; 7:27; 9:18). The disembodied spirit goes to Hades when it is separated from the body at death. Job describes death as a dark, gloomy place from which man cannot return (Job 17:13, 16; 7:9; 10:21).The Old Testament implies that *sheol* has two compartments, one for the wicked and one for the righteous.

For the wicked:

- A place of sorrows (2 Sam. 22:6; Ps. 18:5)
- A place of the wicked (Ps. 9:17)
- A place where the wicked are consumed as water in a drought (Job 24:19)

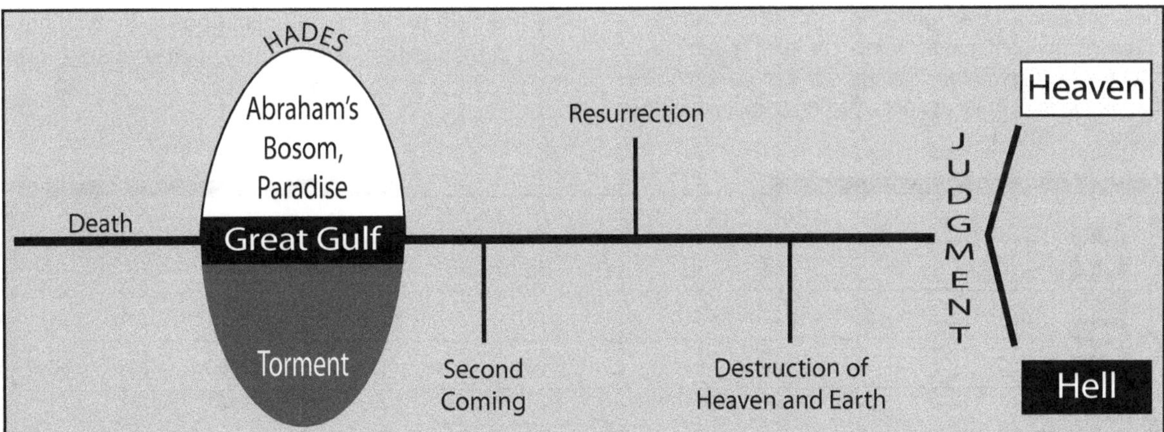

This chart leaves an impression that there is a wide gap of time between the second coming, resurrection, destruction of the heavens and earth, and judgment. That is not its intention, since these events happen so near to each other that one cannot separate them.

- Opposite to the way of life (Prov. 15:24)

For the righteous:

- A place for the dead Messiah (Ps. 16:10)
- Men will awake from *sheol* with God's likeness (Ps. 17:15)
- God will redeem man's soul from *sheol* (Ps. 49:15)
- God will receive the righteous in glory (Ps. 73:24, 25)
- A place of protection (Job 14:13;
- Job expected release from there (Job 14:13; 19:25)

Luke 16:19-31: A Picture of Hades

The Greek New Testament uses the word *hades* to describe the habitation of the dead that is described in the Old Testament by the Hebrew word *sheol*.[1] *Hades* is derived from *Hades* or Pluto, the god of the lower regions. The word was used to describe "the nether world, the realm of the dead.... In the Sept. the Hebr. *šĕʾôl* is almost always rendered by this word.... it denotes, therefore, in bibl. Grk. *Orcus, the infernal regions....* the common receptacle of disembodied spirits" (Thayer, 11).

The most complete description of *hades* is found in Jesus' teaching on the rich man and Lazarus (Luke 16:19-31). The description of this place involves the following things:

- It is a place for both the righteous and the wicked.
- The dead are conscious, having their identity, memory, and desires.
- The dead recognize one another.

[1] The KJV translates several words by the English word "hell," including *hades, gehenna,* and *sheol.* What is meant by the common perception of "hell" is derived from the word *gehenna.* Therefore, we must recognize that *hades* and *sheol* are not referring to hell but to the realm of the dead.

- The wicked are in a place called torment (16:22).
- The righteous are in a place called "Abraham's bosom" (16:23).
- The two places are separated by a great gulf (16:26).
- The dead are not able to pass to or from torment or Abraham's bosom (16:26).
- One's eternal destiny is, therefore, sealed at death.
- The dead are conscious of events on earth (16:27-28).

Other passages allude to the spirit's continued existence after the death of the body:

1. 2 Peter 2:4, 9. "For if God spared not the angels that sinned, but cast them down to hell (from the Greek word *tartaroō*), and delivered them into chains of darkness, to be reserved unto judgment; ... The Lord knoweth how to deliver the godly out of temptations, and to reserve the unjust unto the day of judgment to be punished." Just as the angels that sinned are placed in chains of darkness to await judgment, so also are the unjust reserved for a day of judgment.

2. Luke 23:42-43. Jesus promised the thief on the cross that he would be with him in "paradise" in the day of his death. Jesus went down into *hades* at his death (Ps. 16:10); therefore, paradise is equivalent to "Abraham's bosom" in Luke 16:19-31.

3. Philippians 1:21-23. Paul expected life to continue following the death of his body in which condition he would be in the presence of the Lord.

4. 2 Corinthians 5:1-10. The spirit is not destroyed by the perishing body (2 Cor. 4:16-17). At the moment of death, the spirit goes to be with the Lord in a condition in which the spirit is absent from the body but at home with the Lord (2 Cor. 5:8).

NOTES

5. 1 Thessalonians 4:14-18. Those Christians who have passed away are "asleep in Jesus." When he comes again, he will bring them with him. They did not cease to exist.

6. Romans 8:38-39. Death is unable to separate the Christian from the love of God, because at death he goes to be with the Lord where he has continued existence, though separated from his body.

NOTES

Questions

1. What happens to both the body and soul at death (Eccl. 12:7)? ______

2. Who are depicted in Revelation 6:9 and what were they doing? ______

3. Who are depicted in Revelation 20:4 and what were they doing? ______

4. What limits are placed on man's ability to harm (Matt. 10:28)? ______

5. What can God do to inflict suffering on man that man cannot inflict on others (Matt. 10:28)? ______

6. Answer these questions based on Luke 16:19-31:
   a. What continued to exist beyond death for both the rich man and Lazarus? ______
   b. What was the place of comfort called? ______
   c. What was the place of punishment called? ______
   d. What is the significance of the separating gulf? ______
   e. Why should one conclude that the state of neither could be changed after death? ______

7. Based on 2 Peter 2:4-9, answer these questions:
   a. What became of the angels who sinned? ______
   b. What will become of men who die separated from God? ______

8. What did the Lord promise the thief on the cross (Luke 23:42-43)? ______

9. What is paradise (Luke 23:42-43)? ______

10. What did Paul expect to happen at his death (Phil. 1:21-23)? ______

11. Why did he consider his death a gain? ______

12. What happens at death (2 Cor. 5:1)? ______

13. What is the condition of a Christian who dies (2 Cor. 5:8)? ______________________________

____

14. How are the dead Christians described (1 Thess. 4:14)? ______________________________

____

15. Why is death unable to separate us from the Lord (Rom. 8:38-39)? ______________________

____

Lesson 4

Reincarnation

A television drama features a man and woman who have an almost magnetic attraction for each other. Each person experiences *de javu*, as only television drama can depict. Later the couple learns, through some mystic, that each is the reincarnation of a spirit that existed years ago. They are attracted to each other because they were lovers in their previous cycle of life. Although romantics love the story, it is filled with pagan concepts.

As eastern religions invade the United States, the doctrine of reincarnation spreads. It is important for us to understand what the doctrine of reincarnation is and how it contradicts the revealed word of God in the Bible.

What Is "Reincarnation"?

"Reincarnation" is defined as "the supposed translation of the soul after death into another substance or body than that which it occupied before" (McClintock & Strong, *Cyclopedia of Biblical, Theological, and Ecclesiastical Literature* X: 524). Sometimes reincarnation is referred to as the transmigration of souls.

McClintock and Strong continue, "So long, therefore, as the soul has not attained the condition of purity, it must be born again after the dissolution of the body to which it was allied: and the degree of its impurity at one of these various deaths determines the existence which it will assume in a subsequent life" (Ibid., 525).

McClintock and Strong: "So long, therefore, as the soul has not attained the condition of purity, it must be born again after the dissolution of the body to which it was allied: and the degree of its impurity at one of these various deaths determines the existence which it will assume in a subsequent life."

John B. Noss wrote about reincarnation as follows:

> In its Indo-Aryan form it runs like this: the soul of a man who dies does not, except in the single case of one who at death returns into indistinguishable oneness with Brahman, pass into a permanent state of being in heaven or hell or elsewhere; the soul, rather, is reborn into another existence that will terminate in due time and necessitate yet another birth. Rebirth follows rebirth, with the one exception named, in an endless chain. The successive births are not likely to be on the same plane of being. Rebirth may occur for a finite period of time in any of the series of heavens or hells, or upon earth in any of the forms of life, vegetable, animal, or human. It may thus be either higher or lower than the present or any past existence. A man of low social status now may be reborn as a rajah or a Brahmin, or which is more likely, as an out-caste, or even as an animal, a beetle, worm, vegetable, or soul in hell (*Man's Religions*, 106-107).

Everett L. Cattel made these comments about reincarnation:

> Two other essential concepts are the doctrines of *karma* (works) and transmigration. The laws of moral action are immutable. Wrong actions inevitably produce punishment, and good actions their reward. This is inescapable in an almost fatalistic sense, and to talk of forgiveness or the canceling of sin is completely unrealistic and does injustice to the noble moral law of cause and effect essential in the universe. Whatever of ill one bears in this life is the product of wrong action in a previous existence, and life's blessings come from the good that was done. Our works set off reactions as cause and effect and they must work themselves out to the bitter end. Salvation consists, not of having this canceled or interfered with, but through doing enough good gradually to evolve toward the highest, where one may

> then experience the enlightenment that we are essentially God. In Him there are no distinctions, even of good and evil, and thus one escapes from the ceaseless round of rebirths ("Hinduism," *Religions in a Changing World*, Howard F. Vos, editor, 200).

Hence, reincarnation is not an isolated idea that may be innocently accepted. Reincarnation is one doctrine in a non-Christian, pagan philosophy of life (Hinduism and Buddhism). It is part of a non-Christian religion that is full of idolatry and many false beliefs. It is tied to its own concept of works (*karma*) and its own concept of salvation (*nirvana*).

The Law of Karma

F. LaGard Smith wrote about the law of *karma* that governs reincarnation, "The doctrine of karma teaches that each soul is working its way to perfection by overcoming imperfections in previous lives. Based upon the clearly accurate observation that no one in this present life is perfect, it is correctly assumed that a person cannot, on his own, reach perfection in a single lifetime. The fallacious conclusion is then drawn that it must take many lifetimes in order for each soul to achieve that goal" (*Out on a Broken Limb,* 71).

Understanding *karma* is essential to a proper understanding of reincarnation. Karma teaches these two things: (a) The soul can evolve upward toward perfection until it finally reaches Nirvana (the merging of the soul with the universal soul or universe). (b) The soul can evolve downward. As the soul travels its cycle of re-birth, it evolves upward or downward based on whether one did good or evil in his lifetime. The logical consequences of accepting *karma* and reincarnation are important.

Souls are not confined to human bodies. Souls inhabit every life form. A mouse has a soul of someone who has not progressed very highly on the way to nirvana or who, because of some great wickedness, suffered a regression. That mouse you kill with D-con may be your grandfather or that spider you kill may be your mother-in-law reincarnated. You can understand why scrupulous Hindu ascetics sweep the path in front of them as they walk lest they step on some animal and kill it.

The Law of Karma and the Indian Caste System

The Hindu society in which reincarnation has thrived is a strict caste society. It is defined and defended by the law of *karma* and the reincarnation of souls. During the period around 500 B.C., the caste system was gradually developed. Over the years it evolved into these following five ranks: (a) Brahmins, (b) Kshatriyas, (c) Vaisyas, (d) Shudras. The last group (e) is the "out-castes," the untouchables. These were the dregs of society, unclean and without any hope of ever rising in the social scale. Over the centuries, these five groups have fissured into many sub-castes, each forbidding intermarriage with the other. Note how the caste system is tied to the religious doctrine of *karma*, according to Noss:

> When the caste system was linked up with the Law of Karma, the inequalities of life had at once a simple and comprehensive explanation. The existence of caste in the social structures immediately acquired a kind of moral justification. If a man was born a Shudra, it was because he had sinned in previous existence and deserved no better lot. A Brahmin, on the other hand, had every right to exalt his position and prerogatives; by good deeds in previous existences he had merited his present high station.... The social consequences of the moral justification of caste was apparent in another direction. Any attempt to level up the inequalities of society and lay a broader basis for social justice and reward now became either

NOTES

> **"The social consequences of the moral justification of caste was apparent in another direction. Any attempt to level up the inequalities of society and lay a broader basis for social justice and reward now became either impious or morally wrong-headed. To question the operations of the Law of Karma, as fixing the just retribution for deeds in former lives, became the rankest of heresies" (Noss, 108).**

> impious or morally wrong-headed. To question the operations of the Law of Karma, as fixing the just retribution for deeds in former lives, became the rankest of heresies (Noss, 108).

You can understand why one reaches the conclusion that the law of *karma* and reincarnation are not harmless little doctrines for the rich and idle to play with. Here are some of the consequences of the law of *karma*.

1. The law of *karma* leads to *fatalism.* A person must accept his human condition because it is the repayment of how his soul lived in a previous existence. If he is in a lower caste in India, he should accept it rather than try to improve his station in life. In contrast, the Scriptures teach human initiative: "Whatsoever thy hand findeth to do, do it with thy might" (Eccl. 9:10). Just as laziness leads to poverty, diligent work leads to prosperity (Prov. 6:6-10).

2. The law of *karma* teaches a faulty responsibility for one's actions. Every wrong deed will be accounted for, but not before the Judge of all the earth (Rom. 14:12; 2 Cor. 5:10). Rather, it will be accounted for in the next cycle of the soul's existence. A person yet to be born will reap what you sow.

3. The law of *karma* is a form of legalism. "Salvation" (defined as reaching *nirvana*) is attained through works. There is no concept of forgiveness. In contrast, Paul wrote, "For by grace are ye saved through faith; and that not of yourselves: it is the gift of God: not of works, lest any man should boast" (Eph. 2:8-9). "Salvation" through works is the concept behind reincarnation and the law of *karma*.

The Bible and Reincarnation

1. The concept of the soul in reincarnation differs from that taught in the Bible. The differences are as follows: *(a) The soul has pre-existence.* The Christian believes that the soul begins at birth (or at the moment of conception) and from that point on has immortality. Reincarnation teaches that the soul exists before it inhabits the body and continues to exist after its death to inhabit one body after another until it reaches *nirvana.* Jesus was the only soul on earth to have pre-existence and that because he was the incarnate God. *(b) A soul exists in plants and animals, as well as in man.* Reincarnation teaches that the soul can inhabit any plant or animal. The Bible teaches that man alone has a spirit made in the image of God (Gen. 1:26). *(c) A soul ceases to have separate existence when it attains nirvana.* In contrast to this, the Bible teaches that God made the soul immortal and it will continue to exist in either heaven or hell after this life is over.

2. There is but one cycle of life and death for man. Hebrews 9:27 teaches, "And as it is appointed unto men *once* to die, but after this the judgment." When a man dies, this is the end of his

NOTES

earthly existence. The wise man wrote about the dead saying, "neither have they any more a portion *for ever* in any thing that is done under the sun" (Eccl. 9:6). The story of the rich man and Lazarus shows what happens to man's soul at death. It goes to the hadean world which limits its activity (Luke 16:19-31). At the end of time, there will be a judgment based on the works done in the one body which the soul has inhabited (Rom. 14:12; 2 Cor. 5:10; Rev. 20:11-14). The judgment will not feature God calling one soul to account by saying, "Will the one soul that inhabited a pink rose, a mouse, a dog, a lion, Esau, Manasseh, John Smith, Mary Jones, Peter Clark, Paul Mitchell, etc., ... come to judged?" There is but one life on earth for each person.

3. The law of *karma* is a different law of human accountability. In contrast to a system of legal works, the Bible teaches both law and grace. Consequently, the Lord's grace teaches the possibility of forgiveness for sins committed (Eph. 2:8-10; John 3:16). Salvation in heaven is available to the very chiefest of sinners (1 Tim. 1:15). In contrast, reincarnation is a pessimistic doctrine of strict retribution for sins committed, without any grace to forgive man's wickedness. One pays for his sins by his reincarnation into another body to endure the problems of earth-life again and again.

Reincarnation is a false explanation of the problem of human suffering.

Reincarnation demands that all of sin's punishments must be paid for on earth. In contrast, the Bible teaches that not all accounts of sin are settled on earth. The wicked do prosper (see Eccl. 8:9-10; Ps. 73). The Lord's justice is settled in the judgment, not through an endless cycle of reincarnation. The Lord never explained Job's suffering to be a result of wickedness committed in a previous existence. Reincarnation is a false explanation of the problem of human suffering.

4. Reincarnation denies the resurrection. Like first century pagans thought, modern reincarnation denies the resurrection and does not desire it. The goal of reincarnation is liberation from the body. Why should those who believe in reincarnation desire to see the resurrection of the body in an immortal form? The Christian doctrine, by contrast, is that the body will be raised from the dead and clothed with immortality (1 Cor. 15:42-44). Those who deny the resurrection have undermined the entire Christian faith, including the doctrine of the resurrection of Christ (1 Cor. 15:1-19). Modern believers in reincarnation are like the audience at Athens that heard Paul and mocked (Acts 17:32). They neither believe in nor desire the resurrection from the dead.

5. The eastern concept of reincarnation has a different "heaven." *Nirvana* is the escape from the cycle of reincarnation by the soul's merging with the soul of the universe. It is generally compared to a drop of rain merging with the ocean when it falls into the sea. This is a totally different concept from the Bible concept of "heaven" (Rev. 21).

Conclusion

The next time you watch a TV special that glorifies the eastern concept of reincarnation, I hope that you will be able to identify it as pagan religion. It is a religious system at war with Christianity. The two cannot peacefully co-exist. We also hope that you can identify some of the tenets of the system of religion from which it came and see the conclusions that logically follow should it be accepted.

NOTES

Questions

1. Define "reincarnation": ______________________________

____

2. Why is the cycle of reincarnation necessary? ______________________________

____

3. According to reincarnation, in what forms may a soul be reborn? ______________________________

____

4. According to reincarnation, what is the explanation of:

   a. One's present station in life? ______________________________

   b. The good and evil he experiences in life? ______________________________

5. What is the "law of karma"? ______________________________

____

6. How is it related to reincarnation? ______________________________

____

7. How is India's caste system related to the law of karma? ______________________________

____

8. How does the law of karma and reincarnation lead to fatalism? ______________________________

____

9. What does Ecclesiastes 9:10 teach about changing one's station in life? ______________________________

____

10. How does one give account for his sins according to the law of karma? ______________________________

____

11. How does one give account for his sins according to God's word? ______________________________

____

12. How does one obtain forgiveness in the law of karma? ______________________________

____

13. How does the law of karma conflict with the doctrine of grace (Eph. 2:8-9)? ______________________________

____

14. List three areas in which the doctrine of reincarnation differs from the Bible with reference to the soul:

    a. ______________________________

    b. ______________________________

    c. ______________________________

15. Explain how the following verses conflict with reincarnation:

    a. Hebrews 9:27 — ______________________________

    b. Ecclesiastes 9:6 — ______________________________

16. What happened to the souls of the wicked and dead in Luke 16:19-31? ______________________________

    ____

17. What is the goal of the soul according to reincarnation? ______________________________

    ____

18. What is the Christian's hope? ______________________________

    ____

19. How is reincarnation a denial of the resurrection (1 Cor. 15)? ______________________________

    ____

Lesson 5

The Doctrine of Purgatory

The Roman Catholic[1] doctrine of Purgatory is part of a theological system. Like the Eastern doctrine of reincarnation, one cannot fully understand that doctrine without understanding how it fits into the Roman Catholic concept of salvation.

The Roman Catholic Doctrine of Purgatory

Purgatory is the place where the soul of man is cleansed from the vestiges of sin that were not cleansed on earth. Here are the statements of the Catholic doctrine taken from their own books:

> That punishment or the vestiges of sin may remain to be expiated or cleansed and that they in fact frequently do even after the remission of guilt[2] is clearly demonstrated by the doctrine of purgatory. In purgatory, in fact, the souls of those "who died in the charity of God and truly repentant, but before satisfying with worthy fruits of penance for sins committed and for omissions" are cleansed after death with purgatorial punishments (*The Catechism of Modern Man*, compiled and edited by a Team of Daughters of St. Paul, 622).

The Catholic Church has defined the existence of Purgatory in the Decree of Union drawn up at the Council of Florence in 1439, and again at the Council of Trent (Sess. xxv.) which says: "The Catholic Church, instructed by the Holy Ghost, has from Sacred Scriptures, and the ancient traditions of the Fathers, taught in Sacred Councils, and very recently in this Ecumenical Synod (Sess. vi., can. 30; Sess. xxii., chs. 2, 3) that there is a Purgatory, and that the souls therein detained are helped by the suffrages of the faithful, but principally by the acceptable sacrifice of the altar."

In Roman Catholic doctrine, Purgatory is the place where the soul of man is cleansed from the vestiges of sin that were not cleansed on earth.

The same Council taught (Sess. xiv., can. 12), in accordance with the Scriptures (Num. xx. 12; 2 Kings xii. 13, 14) that God does not always remit all of the temporal punishment due to forgiven sin. The Scriptures teach that nothing defiled can enter heaven (Wisd. vii. 25; Isa. xxv. 8; Hab. i. 13; Apoc. xxi. 7), and that Christians often die with venial sins upon their souls. All, therefore, who die in venial sins, or with the temporal punishment of their sins still unpaid must atone for them in Purgatory (Bertrand L. Conway, *The Question Box,* 393-394).

The Catholic doctrine is most reasonable. It follows logically from the fact that many die with the burden of venial sins on their conscience, or die with the temporal punishment due to their forgiven sins still unpaid. The average Christian commits many a venial sin in his lifetime, for which he never craves pardon. The sinner of many years standing,

---

[1] The Roman Catholics are not the only ones who believe in purgatory. The eastern branch of the Catholic church, the Greek Orthodox Church, also accepts most of the same beliefs about purgatory. Orthodox Judaism also accepts a version of purgatory. According to the *Talmud*, "those who die in communion with the synagogue, or who have never been Jews, are punished for twelve months, but that Jewish heretics and apostates are doomed to eternal punishment" (M'Clintock and Strong, *Cyclopedia of Biblical, Theological, and Ecclesiastical Literature,* VIII: 798).

[2] The Roman Catholics are not the only ones who believe in purgatory. The eastern branch of the Catholic church, the Greek Orthodox Church, also accepts most of the same beliefs about purgatory. Orthodox Judaism also accepts a version of purgatory. According to the *Talmud*, "those who die in communion with the synagogue, or who have never been Jews, are punished for twelve months, but that Jewish heretics and apostates are doomed to eternal punishment" (M'Clintock and Strong, *Cyclopedia of Biblical, Theological, and Ecclesiastical Literature* VIII:798).

[2] Please notice that the blood of Christ gives remission but does not thoroughly do away with sin, according to this Catholic author.

who in God's mercy is pardoned on his deathbed, must in the hereafter, unless given a plenary indulgence, satisfy to the last farthing his debt of temporal punishment (*Ibid.,* 396).

For each one of us there is a special judgment immediately after death.... If the divine life in our soul is unrestricted, it will be transformed at once into glory, and we will see God face to face. If our sanctity has spots and blemishes, we will be painfully aware of them and see how they delay our eventual happiness.

The Catholic doctrine of purgatory is intertwined with several others Catholic doctrinal errors.

In the particular judgment, the person who loves God completely will follow the lead of his love directly to heaven. The person who does not love God, or who loves creatures more, will end up in hell. And those who love God essentially, but not completely, must purify the defects of their love before they are ready for heaven.

There is no opportunity for repentance after death, but there is a place of purification and a method of expiation. We call it purgatory. You and I may be reasonably sure right now that we have the life of grace in our souls; but we must also be aware that we harbor venial sins which have never been fully repented, weaknesses which cripple our love, and a residue of past sins never completely expiated.... we realize that we are just not fit for the holiness of heaven; we would feel uncomfortable among the saints, embarrassed in the presence of God.

But heaven knows no discomfort. So we delay in purgatory long enough to rub off, by suffering, the spots left by sin, long enough to burn away, in the intensity of God's love, the various remains of sin. Purgatory loosens the devious attachments of our wills, that we may fix themselves unhindered on God. It fits us to be welcome in heaven, equips us to enjoy it fully (J.D. Conway, *Facts of the Faith,* 351-352).

These Catholic scholars explain to us what Purgatory is. Purgatory is "a purgatorial fire, where the souls of the righteous are purified by a temporary punishment [*ad definitum tempus cruciatæ expiantur*], that entrance may be given them into their eternal home, where nothing that is defiled can have a place" (M'Clintock and Strong VIII: 795).

The Catholic doctrine of purgatory is intertwined with several other Catholic doctrinal errors. Particularly one must understand the following:

1. Mortal and venial sin. Mortal sins are sins that drive sanctifying grace completely out of the soul; so the soul is dead supernaturally; spiritual death results from the soul's complete separation from the love of God. *Venial sins* are not deadly; they merely wound and cripple the effectiveness of our supernatural life. They do not cause one to lose heaven or go to hell. (See James 2:11 and Romans 6:23 to see that all sin has the same consequence of separation of the soul from God.)

2. The role of the Catholic Church to grant absolution. In Catholic theology, the church is God's divine agent to dispense grace to man. The church has the power to "absolve" one from his sins, that is to grant forgiveness of sins.

3. Penance. In the concept of penance, "we deny ourselves, accept sufferings, and perform strenuous works in an effort to expiate our guilt" (Conway, *Facts of the Faith,* 192). "... the penitent confesses his sins, expresses his sorrow, and proposes to make satisfaction for his sins; and the priest, representing Christ, speaks the judgment of forgiveness" (*Ibid.*). In penance one pays for his sins by undergoing some temporal penalty,

NOTES

as a token payment for the harm one's sins have done. Penance remits a portion of the temporal punishments for sin.

4. Indulgences. Indulgences are used by the Catholic Church to "forgive the temporal punishments which remain after penance has done its work.... an indulgence is the forgiveness of punishment which God's justice still demands in many cases after sins have been forgiven" (Conway, *Facts of the Faith,* 220, 222). Indulgences can be granted because saints through the years have accumulated an abundance of merit from their good works that can be applied to an individual's account, the Catholic Church being God's dispenser of these merits. Indulgences are available both for the living and the dead. "We might say that the Church, in granting an indulgence for the souls in purgatory, presents to Almighty God her rich treasury of merits and satisfactions centered around the sacrifice of the Cross; and in her official capacity as the representative of Christ on earth, she asks God to liberate the souls in purgatory from some of their sufferings" (*Ibid.,* 225).

5. Prayer for the dead. Those in purgatory are relieved of their suffering by the prayers of their fellow-members here on earth, also by alms and masses offered up to God for their souls. The Council of Trent taught that "the Mass is a propitiatory Sacrifice for the living and the dead, and that the souls in Purgatory are helped by the suffrages of the faithful, but chiefly by the acceptable Sacrifice of the Altar" (Conway, *The Question Box,* 270).

Putting these ideas together, one comes up with a theological system that works like this: An individual who was a pretty good person, but not a saint, dies. His soul does not go to heaven, but to purgatory. There he must burn until his sins are purged from his soul. His living relatives and the Catholic Church can offer prayers in his behalf and have Masses said to shorten his purgatorial punishment. The loving survivors pay for Masses to be offered and indulgences so that his stay in purgatory can be shortened.[3]

How Purgatory Is Defended

1. 2 Maccabees 12:43-46. 1 and 2 Maccabees are two of fifteen books in the Catholic Bible that are not in the Protestant Bible. They are called *apocryphal books.* Protestants do not believe that they are inspired books because they were not among the accepted canon of the Old Testament that was used by Jesus and the first century Jews. The text in 2 Maccabees says,

> And when he had made a gathering throughout the company to the sum of two thousand drachmas of silver, he sent it to Jerusalem to offer a sin offering, doing therein very well and honestly, in that he was mindful of the resurrection: for if he had not hoped that they that were slain should have risen again, it had been superfluous and vain to *pray for the dead.* And also in that he perceived that there was great favour laid up for those that died godly, it was an holy and good thought. Whereupon, *he made a reconciliation for the dead, that they might be delivered from sin.*

The context of this is one of Judas' Maccabees battles in which some of the valiant Jews who died fighting for Israel's independence and freedom to offer worship in the Temple were found with things consecrated to idols in their possession. Because this was a sin, he took up a collection for the offering described above.

Inasmuch as 2 Maccabees is not inspired Scripture, it provides no authority for sacrifices for

[3] Even Catholic historians admit that this system was abused in the Reformation era when the sale of indulgences became a lucrative means of raising huge sums of money.

NOTES

the dead. If this passage proves anything, it proves that animal sacrifices for the dead were offered in the Jewish Temple and says nothing about saying Masses in the Roman Catholic Church.

Inasmuch as 2 Maccabees is not inspired Scripture, it provides no authority for sacrifices for the dead.

2. *Matthew 5:25.* "Agree with thine adversary quickly, whiles thou art in the way with him; lest at any time the adversary deliver thee to the judge, and the judge deliver thee to the officer, and thou be cast into prison." Catholics interpret the "prison" of this passage to refer to purgatory. It is not speaking of purgatory but emphasizing the hopelessness of an eternal damnation.

3. *Matthew 12:32.* "And whosoever speaketh a word against the Son of man, it shall be forgiven him: but whosoever speaketh against the Holy Ghost, it shall not be forgiven him, neither in this world, neither in the world to come." Catholics argue that there are some sins that will be forgiven men "in the world to come" (meaning after death). Jesus is using "the world to come" in its typical Jewish sense of the Messianic age, the Christian dispensation. He is saying that one who blasphemes God by rejecting the divinely revealed word can never be forgiven, neither in the Jewish age nor the Messianic age. In contrast, one who rejected Jesus during his earthly life, may be converted after the resurrection, but one who rejects the divinely revealed revelation by the Holy Spirit can never be forgiven.

4. *1 Corinthians 3:11-15.* This passage is understood to describe purgatory in the phrase "he himself shall be saved; yet so as by fire" (3:15). This passage is not speaking about one's sins being cleansed after death. Rather, it is speaking of how the fire tests one's earthly works, to see of what sort it is. "If any man's work abide which he hath built thereupon, he shall receive a reward" (3:14). The work that a preacher does in teaching others the gospel will be tested. Those who are converted will be tested by the fires of temptation to see if they remain faithful. Some who are lost will be lost because of the wrong kind of work that was done by the preacher; others will be lost in spite of the best work that one can do. Those whose works are so destroyed nevertheless will be saved.

5. *Revelation 21:27.* "And there shall in no wise enter into it any thing that defileth, neither whatsoever worketh abomination, or maketh a lie: but they which are written in the Lamb's book of life." This passage speaks not a word about purgatory. Rather, it simply states that those whose sins have not been forgiven will not have eternal life.

What Is Wrong with Purgatory

1. The doctrine of purgatory is not taught in the Scriptures. Inasmuch as there is no clear teaching about purgatory in the Scriptures, one who teaches it has gone beyond the doctrine of Christ (1 Cor. 4:6; 2 John 9-11). The Scriptures describe a two-fold receptacle for souls: (a) Abraham's bosom (Luke 16:22) or paradise (Luke 23:43) and (b) Torment (Luke 16:28). There is no Bible teaching of a third receptacle for souls known as purgatory.

M'Clintock and Strong wrote, "But whatever the views of Church fathers on the subject, as a doctrine it was unknown in the Christian Church for the first 600 years, and it does not appear to have been made an article of faith until the 10th century" (VIII: 796).

NOTES

2. The concept of purgatory is part of a theological system of salvation by meritorious works. The forgiveness obtained by the blood of Christ is not sufficient to thoroughly cleanse one's soul (contrast to 1 John 1:7). Rather, one's soul must be cleansed by temporal suffering from sin and penance. Hence, one obtains entrance into heaven by undergoing this suffering from sin and doing those things the priest demands for penance. No man has "meritorious works" that can be transferred from one believer's account to another, as is done in the sale of indulgences and invocation of the saints.

3. Purgatory offers a false hope to those who die in disobedience to the Lord. Those who die unforgiven of their sins are lost. There is no second chance, such as the Catholic doctrine of purgatory offers, in which one's soul is purged of sins after death.

4. Purgatory is part of a theological system that makes the Roman Catholic Church the dispenser of salvation. In Roman Catholicism, the apostle Peter is believed to have been the first pope and to him was given the divine power to absolve sin, which power was transmitted in an unbroken line of popes unto this day. The Catholic Church, as the recipient of this power invested in its priests, can absolve sin.

5. The doctrine of purgatory attacks the all-sufficiency of the atonement. Catholic scholars state that the atonement forgives sin but does not pay for the temporal consequences of sin. All sins have temporal consequences that must be paid before one can enter heaven. Some are paid while on earth (through penance and indulgences) and the rest must be paid in purgatory.

NOTES

Questions

1. Name three religions that believe in purgatory. ______________________

____

2. What is "purgatory"? ______________________
3. According to Romans Catholicism,
   a. What is mortal sin? ______________________
   b. What is venial sin? ______________________
   c. What is the role of the church in forgiving sin? ______________________
   d. What is penance? ______________________
   e. What are indulgences? ______________________
   f. What is the treasure from which indulgences are granted? ______________________
   g. What is prayer for the dead? ______________________
4. What does James 2:11 say about the differences in sin? ______________________

____

5. What are the wages of sin (Rom. 6:23)? ______________________
6. What is 2 Maccabees? ______________________
7. Why do we not accept it as authoritative? ______________________

____

8. List the verses Catholics generally use to defend the doctrine of purgatory: ______________________

____

9. What does Luke 16:19-31 show regarding the state of:
   a. The righteous dead? ______________________
   b. The partially righteous dead? ______________________
   c. The wicked? ______________________
10. What does Luke 16:19-31 show about one's ability to change his eternal sentence after death?

____

11. In what way does the doctrine of purgatory relate to salvation by works? ______________________

____

12. What hope does purgatory give to unforgiven sinners who die? ______________________
13. What role does the Roman Catholic Church assume with reference to forgiveness of sins? ______________________

____

The Second Coming

The New Testament teaches that Christians live between two blessed events: (1) The first coming of Jesus at the incarnation when an atonement for sin was made and (2) The second coming of Jesus when he comes for his saints. There is only one time in Scripture when Jesus' coming at the end of the age is described as his "second" coming. That appears as follows:

> And as it is appointed unto men once to die, but after this the judgment: so Christ was once offered to bear the sins of many; and unto them that look for him *shall he appear the second time* without sin unto salvation (Heb. 9:27-28).

This lesson is designed to study the second coming of Jesus. The Scriptures speak of the "coming of the Lord" in a whole host of passages (1 Cor. 1:7; 15:23; 1 Thess. 2:19; 3:13; 4:15; 5:23; 2 Thess. 2:1, 8; 2 Pet. 3:12).

There can be no doubt that the New Testament speaks of the Lord's coming and that Christians are to live in expectation of that coming. Jesus promised that he would come again in the following passages:

1. John 14:1-6. "Let not your heart be troubled: ye believe in God, believe also in me. In my Father's house are many mansions: if it were not so, I would have told you. I go to prepare a place for you. And if I go and prepare a place for you, *I will come again, and receive you unto myself*; that where I am, there ye may be also" (John 14:1-3). Later, Jesus explained that man has access to the Father only through him saying, "I am the way, the truth, and the life: no man cometh unto the Father, but by me" (John 14:6). Those who "come to the Father" must come through Christ. Jesus promised to come again and receive unto himself those who did come to the Father through him.

2. Acts 1:11. The angels announced to those who witnessed Jesus ascend into heaven that he would come again saying, "Ye men of Galilee, why stand ye gazing up into heaven? This same Jesus, which is taken up from you into heaven, shall so come in like manner as ye have seen him go into heaven."

"Ye men of Galilee, why stand ye gazing up into heaven? This same Jesus, which is taken up from you into heaven, shall so come in like manner as ye have seen him go into heaven" (Acts 1:11).

3. 1 Corinthians 4:5. "Therefore judge nothing before the time, *until the Lord come*, who both will bring to light the hidden things of darkness, and will make manifest the counsels of the hearts: and then shall every man have praise of God." Paul promised the Corinthians that the Lord would come and, at that time, the secrets of men's hearts would be judged.

4. 1 Thessalonians 4:15-17. "For this we say unto you by the word of the Lord, that we which are alive and remain unto *the coming of the Lord* shall not prevent them which are asleep. For the Lord himself shall descend from heaven with a shout, with the voice of the archangel, and with the trump of God: and the dead in Christ shall rise first: Then we which are alive and remain shall be caught up together with them in the clouds, to meet the Lord in the air: and so shall we ever be with the Lord." This passage promises that the dead saints will be raised when the Lord Jesus comes again.

5. 2 Thessalonians 1:7-10. "And to you who are troubled rest with us, when the Lord Jesus shall be revealed from heaven with his mighty angels, in flaming fire taking vengeance on them that know not God, and that obey not the gospel of our Lord Jesus Christ: who shall be punished with everlasting destruction from the presence of the Lord, and from the glory of his power; when he shall come to be glorified in his saints, and to be admired in all them that believe (because our testimony among you was believed) in that day." At the revelation of the Lord Jesus, the saints will have rest, the wicked will be punished in flaming fire, and Christ shall be glorified in his saints.

6. Hebrews 10:37. Writing to encourage the Hebrew Christians to persevere in their faith in spite of affliction, the writer of Hebrews promised, "For yet a little while, and he that shall come will come, and will not tarry."

7. Jude 14-15. "And Enoch also, the seventh from Adam, prophesied of these, saying, Behold, the Lord cometh with ten thousands of his saints, to execute judgment upon all, and to convince all that are ungodly among them of all their ungodly deeds which they have ungodly committed, and of all their hard speeches which ungodly sinners have spoken against him." Notice that the Lord's coming destroys *all* the ungodly.

8. Revelation 1:7. "Behold, he cometh with clouds; and every eye shall see him, and they also which pierced him: and all kindreds of the earth shall wail because of him. Even so, Amen." When Jesus comes, "every eye shall see him."

Terms by Which His Coming Is Described

1. Apocalypse. The word *apocalypse* is the transliteration of *apokalupsis* which means "an uncovering." It is used of the revelation of the hidden will of God on many occasions (Eph. 3:3, for example). It is also used "of events by which things or states or persons hitherto withdrawn from view are made visible to all, *manifestation, appearance*" (Thayer, 62). In this sense, the second coming of Jesus is called the *apokalupsis tou kurious Iesou Christou* in these passages: 1 Corinthians 1:7; 2 Thessalonians 1:7; 1 Peter 1:7, 13. By its very definition, the Lord's second coming cannot be something hidden and secret. It is a "revelation" of the Lord Jesus.

2. Epiphany is used to describe the Lord's coming. It means "an appearing, appearance ... often used by the Greeks of a glorious manifestation of the gods, and esp. of their advent to help.... In the N.T. the 'advent' of Christ,—not only that which has already taken place and by which his presence and power appear in the saving light he has shed

The Lord's Second Coming is. . .

- **Expected.** The Lord promised to come again!
- **Unexpected.** We do not know when he will return.
- **Certain:** The Lord will do what he said he will do.
- **A Visisble Return.** All eyes will see him.
- **A Personal Return:** Jesus himself will come again.
- **Guaranteed by Jesus' Resurrection.**
- **The End of the Days of Salvation.**
- **The Day of the Resurrection of the Dead.**
- **The Day for Judgment.**
- **The Day of Salvation for the Saved.**
- **The Day of Condemnation for the Lost.**

NOTES

upon mankind ... but also that illustrious return from heaven to earth hereafter to occur" (Thayer, 245-246). This word is used in these texts: 1 Timothy 6:14; 2 Timothy 4:1, 8; Titus 2:13.

3. Parousia is also used to describe the Lord's second coming. The word means "presence" (as opposed to absence), "**2.** the presence of one coming, hence *the coming, arrival, advent....* In the N.T. esp. of *the advent*, i.e. the future, visible, *return* from heaven of Jesus, the Messiah, to raise the dead, hold the last judgment, and set up formally and gloriously the kingdom of God" (Thayer, 490). Although some of the passages cited with this meaning by Thayer may be disputed, the following seem clearly to speak of the Lord's second coming: 1 Corinthians 15:23; 1 Thessalonian 2:19; 3:13; 4:15; 5:23; 2 Thessalonians 2:1, 8; James 5:7; 2 Peter 1:16; 3:4, 12; 1 John 2:28.

4. The day. The phrase "day" is used in a number of phrases to describe the second coming of Christ. The usages are too numerous to list all of them here. Thayer says about the word *hemera* in this usage, "**3.** of *the last day of the present age*, ... the day in which Christ will return from heaven, raise the dead, hold the final judgment, and perfect his kingdom" (Thayer, 278). Here are some of its usages: (a) Day of God (2 Pet. 3:12); (b) Day of the Lord (1 Thess. 5:2); (c) Day of the Lord Jesus (1 Cor. 1:8; Phil. 1:6, 10; 2 Pet. 3:10); (d) "That day" (2 Thess. 1:10; 2 Tim. 1:12, 18); (e) The Last Day (John 6:39-54); (f) The Great Day (Rom. 2:5); (g) The Day of Redemption (Eph. 4:30); (f) The Day of Wrath (Rom. 2:5); (g) The Day of Judgment (Jude 6); (h) The Day of Revelation (Rev. 6:17). The modifying phrases ("of redemption," "of wrath," "of judgment," "of revelation") point us to the events of the great day of Jesus' coming.

Different "Comings" of the Lord

Looking at the words that are used to refer to the second coming, one can see that the "coming" of the Lord can also be used in reference to other "comings" of the Lord than the "second coming" at the end of time. Understanding that the phrase can be used of comings other than the second coming helps us to explain why the "coming" is sometimes spoken of as "imminent" and sometimes delayed and far removed. The Lord is said to "come" in the following senses:

1. In judgment against Jerusalem. Apocalyptic language, similar to that used in Isaiah, Daniel, Ezekiel, and Zechariah to describe God's judgment against the kingdoms of men, is used in Matthew 24 (and parallels in Mark 13 and Luke 21) to describe the Lord's coming in judgment against Jerusalem (Matt. 24:30). These passages speak of the Lord coming within the lifetime of those present (Matt. 24:34-35).

2. In the establishment of his kingdom. Jesus said, "Verily I say unto you, That there be some of them that stand here, which shall not taste of death, till they have seen the kingdom of God come with power" (Mark 9:1). This prophecy was fulfilled on the day of Pentecost when the apostles received power as the Holy Spirit came upon them (Acts 1:8; 2:1-4). This also came within the lifetime of those who heard Jesus preach.

3. The visible second coming of the Lord in the last day. When the "coming" of the Lord is used of the final second coming, it is spoken of as a day far removed (Matt. 25:5, 19; Mark 2:19-20; 14:7-9; Luke 12:45; 19:11;). The Parables of the Tares (Matt. 13:24-30, 37-43), of the Mustard Seed (Matt. 13:31-32), and of the Leaven (Matt. 13:33) imply a delay between the time Jesus spoke and his second coming.

NOTES

Because the coming was far removed and no one knows when it will occur, there are a number of passages which speak of the Lord's coming with uncertainty as to the time of his coming (Matt. 24:36-39; 25:13; Luke 12:35-40; 1 Thess. 5:2-4, 9-10).

Failure to recognize that there are distinct comings of the Lord has led some to take passages that speak of one specific coming (such as the Lord's coming in judgment against Jerusalem or to establish his kingdom) and apply them to the "second coming," reaching such bizarre conclusions as saying that the Lord's second coming occurred in A.D. 70.

Failure to recognize that there are distinct comings of the Lord has led some to take passages that speak of one specific coming (such as the Lord's coming in judgment against Jerusalem or to establish his kingdom) and apply them to the "second coming," reaching such bizarre conclusions as saying that the Lord's second coming occurred in A.D. 70.

The Manner of His Coming

The passages that speak of the Lord's coming lead us to some conclusions about the manner of Jesus' coming.

1. *It will be a visible return.* It will be witnessed by all men, in contrast to a hidden, secret return. John wrote, "Behold, he cometh with clouds; *and every eye shall see him*, and they also which pierced him: and all kindreds of the earth shall wail because of him. Even so, Amen" (Rev. 1:7). When he comes, men of every nation will be brought before him for judgment (Matt. 25:31-46). His coming will be so public that no one will have to say "lo, here" or "lo, there," for his coming will be as visible as the lightning in the heavens. "For as the lightning, that lighteneth out of the one part under heaven, shineth unto the other part under heaven; so shall also the Son of man be in his day" (Luke 17:24). His second coming will be as visible as his ascension. Here is the announcement of the angels when Jesus ascended into heaven:

> And when he had spoken these things, while they beheld, he was taken up; and a cloud received him out of their sight. And while they looked stedfastly toward heaven as he went up, behold, two men stood by them in white apparel; Which also said, Ye men of Galilee, why stand ye gazing up into heaven? This same Jesus, which is taken up from you into heaven, shall so come in like manner as ye have seen him go into heaven (Acts 1:9-11).

Any teaching that makes the second coming something that is not witnessed by *every eye* is different from that revealed in the word of God.

2. *It will be a glorious coming.* When Jesus made his advent into this world by being born to Mary, he came in humble circumstances. When he comes again, his coming will be glorious.

> For the Son of man shall *come in the glory* of his Father with his angels; and then he shall reward every man according to his works (Matt. 16:27).

> When the Son of man shall *come in his glory*, and all the holy angels with him, then shall he sit upon the throne of his glory (Matt. 25:31).

> For whosoever shall be ashamed of me and of my words, of him shall the Son of man be ashamed, when he shall *come in his own glory*, and in his Father's, and of the holy angels (Luke 9:26).

NOTES

3. His coming will not be preceded by visible signs. In contrast to the signs foretelling the destruction of Jerusalem which the disciples could identify so as to escape the city, when Jesus comes there will be no warning signs. He will come like a "thief in the night" (that is, without warning).

> Watch therefore: for ye know not what hour your Lord doth come. But know this, that if the goodman of the house had known in what watch the thief would come, he would have watched, and would not have suffered his house to be broken up. Therefore be ye also ready: for in such an hour as ye think not the Son of man cometh (Matt. 24:42-44).

> But ye, brethren, are not in darkness, that that day should overtake you as a thief (1 Thess. 5:4).

> But the day of the Lord will come as a thief in the night; in the which the heavens shall pass away with a great noise, and the elements shall melt with fervent heat, the earth also and the works that are therein shall be burned up (2 Pet. 3:10).

His coming will be at an hour unknown to men (Matt. 24:36-51; 25:1-12; 1 Thess. 5:1-3).

The Day of God's Grace Ends When Jesus Comes Again

1. The church in its completeness will be presented to God. The Scriptures teach that when Jesus comes again, the Lord will present to the Father his glorious church. When the Lord comes back, he is not coming to "set up" his kingdom, but to "deliver up" his kingdom to the Father.

> But every man in his own order: Christ the firstfruits; afterward they that are Christ's at his coming. Then cometh the end, when he shall have delivered up the kingdom to God, even the Father; when he shall have put down all rule and all authority and power. For he must reign, till he hath put all enemies under his feet. The last enemy that shall be destroyed is death (1 Cor 15:23-26).

The order of this occurring is revealed. Christ, as the firstfruits of the resurrection, was raised from the dead and ascended to the right hand of God. At "his coming," Christ will "deliver up" the kingdom to the Father, and this will occur only after every power which exalts itself against his authority has been put down. The last enemy that will be destroyed is death.

When the Lord comes back, he is not coming to "set up" his kingdom, but to "deliver up" his kingdom to the Father.

The "glorious church" will be presented to the Father in its pristine purity, having been cleansed by the blood of the Lamb (Eph. 5:25-27; Col. 1:22; 1 Thess. 3:13; 2 Thess. 1:10; Jude 24). When the church is presented to the Father, *it will be complete.* The "fulness of the Gentiles" will have been added to the kingdom (Rom. 11:12, 25). When the church is presented to the Father, *it will be pure.* It will have been cleansed with the "washing of water by the word," it will be "holy and unblameable and unreproveable," it will be "unblameable in holiness," and "faultless." Having been so cleansed, when it is presented to the Father, the church *will be glorious.* David Brown wrote,

> One magnificent conception pervades them all —
>
> The absolute *completeness* of the Church at Christ's coming,
>
> The spotless *purity* in which it will be presented, "as a chaste virgin," to Christ,
>
> The resplendent *glory* in which, as "the Bride, the Lamb's wife," she shall then be "adorned for her Husband,"

NOTES

Events Associated With The Lord's Return

- **The simultaneous resurrection of all the dead, both good and bad (John 5:28-29; 6:40, 44; 11:24; 1 Cor. 15:23; 1 Thess. 4:16; Rev. 20:11-15).**
- **The Judgment of all men (Matt. 7:21, 23; 13:30-43; 16:27; 25:31-46; Acts 17:31).**
- **The destruction of the heavens and earth with fire (Matt. 24:35; Heb. 1:11; 2 Pet. 3:7-13; Rev. 20:11; 21:1).**

> The *praise* which will redound from such a spectacle to the Redeemer himself,
>
> The rapturous *admiration* of Him which it will kindle, and
>
> The ineffable *complacency* with which the whole will be regarded by "God, even our Father" (*Christ's Second Coming* 57).

If the church is complete when it is presented to the Father, there will be no room for later additions after the second coming.[1]

2. All means of grace end at the second coming. All of the incentives to the saints to faithfulness are tied to faithfulness *until Jesus comes* (Luke 19:13; Phil 3:20; James 5:7; 1 Pet. 1:13; Rev. 22:12). The second coming of Christ is mentioned as an incentive for the lost to repent, lest the judgment of the Lord come against them at the second coming (Luke 12:39-40; 17:26-30; 2 Thess. 1:7-10; 2 Pet. 3:10). As Jesus gave the Parable of the Virgins, he succinctly stated that when he came and received the wise virgins to himself, "the door was shut" (Matt. 25:10). *The day of God's grace ends at the Lord's second coming.*

The nature of what occurs when Jesus comes again makes impossible the extending of God's grace after that event. Consider what will occur:

> Because he hath appointed a day, in the which he will judge the world in righteousness by that man whom he hath ordained; whereof he hath given assurance unto all men, in that he hath raised him from the dead (Acts 17:31).
>
> In the day when God shall judge the secrets of men by Jesus Christ according to my gospel (Rom. 2:16).
>
> But the heavens and the earth, which are now, by the same word are kept in store, reserved unto fire against the day of judgment and perdition of ungodly men (2 Pet. 3:7).

When Jesus comes again, the day of judgment will occur for every man. The whole world will be judged, the secrets of men's hearts will be judged, and it will be a day of judgment and perdition for ungodly men. There will be no offer of grace to ungodly men at that day.

3. The Christian ordinances will be over. There are two ordinances peculiar to Christianity, namely the Lord's supper and water baptism. Both of them are designed to last until the Lord's second coming. With reference to the Lord's supper, Paul wrote, "For as often as ye eat this bread, and drink this cup, ye do show the Lord's death *till he come*"

[1] One of the problems of the A.D. 70 view is that it presents the second coming of Christ as occurring in A.D. 70, at which time the church is presented to God. If the church is presented complete to the Father in A.D. 70, then there is no opportunity for others to be added to that church.

NOTES

(1 Cor. 11:26). When Jesus comes back, the eating and drinking of the Lord's supper will end.

Jesus also spoke of baptism as lasting to the "end of the world." He said, "All power is given unto me in heaven and in earth. Go ye therefore, and teach all nations, baptizing them in the name of the Father, and of the Son, and of the Holy Ghost: teaching them to observe all things whatsoever I have commanded you: and, lo, I am with you alway, even unto the end of the world" (Matt. 28:18-20).

4. The Lord's intercessory work in heaven will end. Hebrews 9:12, 24-28 relates that the Lord's intercessory work began when he took his blood into the Holy of Holies in heaven to make intercession for us. Even to this day, he ever lives to make intercession for us (Heb. 7:25). However, when he comes back, he will come back, not to make a sacrifice for sin, but with salvation to those already saved from sin.

> And as it is appointed unto men once to die, but after this the judgment: So Christ was once offered to bear the sins of many; and unto them that look for him shall he appear the second time without sin unto salvation (Heb. 9:27-28).

At that time his intercessory work will be over and he will cease to appear in the presence of God for us. If the second coming occurred in A.D. 70, Christ's intercessory work ended at that time as well. He no longer makes intercession for man or pleads man's case before God (1 John 2:1-2).

Conclusion

The early church lived with a sense of the expectation of the imminence of the Lord's return. They looked forward to it with anxious expectation (1 Cor. 16:22: Rev. 22:20). Anthony Hoekema wrote,

> There may be various reasons for the loss of this sense of expectation. It may be that the church today is caught up in material and secular concerns that interest in the Second Coming is fading into the background. It may be that many Christians no longer believe in a literal return of Christ. It may also be that many who do believe in a literal return have pushed that event so far into the distant future that they no longer live in anticipation of that return. Whatever the reasons may be, the loss of a lively, vital anticipation of the Second Coming of Christ is a sign of a most serious spiritual malady in the church (*The Bible and the Future* 110).

Any teaching that excludes from its hope the belief that Jesus will come again teaches a different hope than the New Testament reveals.

NOTES

Questions

1. Define the following:
   a. Christ's first coming: ____________________
   b. Christ's second coming: ____________________
2. What promise did Jesus give the apostles in John 14:1-6? ____________________
3. What promise did Jesus give the apostles in Acts 1:9-11? ____________________
4. Who will see Christ when he returns (Rev. 1:7)? ____________________
5. Why is Jesus second coming called an "apocalypse"? ____________________
6. Why is Jesus second coming called an "epiphany"? ____________________
7. Why is Jesus second coming called a "parousia"? ____________________
8. List three comings of Christ and tell which were soon to occur and which were far removed:
   a. ____________________
   b. ____________________
   c. ____________________
9. Why does one conclude that Jesus' second coming will be visible? ____________________
10. How will his second coming be like his ascension (Acts 1:9-11)? ____________________
11. Contrast Jesus' first and second coming with reference to their respective glory. ____________________
12. Why is Christ's second coming not preceded by signs (Matt. 24:42-44; 1 Thess. 5:4; 2 Pet. 3:10)? ____________________
13. If the church is complete when Christ comes again, how many can be saved after his coming? ____________________

14. What does the phrase “the door was shut” mean (Matt. 25:10)? ______________________

____

15. What two Christian ordinances will end at the second coming? ______________________

____

16. What three events will occur at the second coming?

    a. ____

    b. ____

    c. ____

17. Why is this generation less conscious of the second coming than were first century saints? _______

____

____

Lesson 7

The Resurrection

The Old Testament and the Resurrection

The doctrine of the resurrection is more fully revealed in the New Testament than it had been in the Old Testament. There were glimpses of the resurrection found in the Old Testament, but not a comprehensive doctrine. In this respect, Jesus brought life and immortality to light through the gospel (2 Tim. 1:10). In Genesis 5:24, Enoch passed from this earth directly to the presence of the Lord, which is probably the first indication of a life beyond this life. Other Old Testament passages reveal the concept of the resurrection in the following texts:

1. Exodus 3:6. Most likely, one would not recognize the implications of this passage had not the Lord Jesus explained them to us. In Matthew 22:29-32, Jesus answered the Sadducees who asked him about the resurrection by appealing to this passage. Exodus 3:6 reads, "Moreover he said, I am the God of thy father, the God of Abraham, the God of Isaac, and the God of Jacob." In commenting on this passage to prove the resurrection of the dead, Jesus said, "Ye do err, not knowing the scriptures, nor the power of God. For in the resurrection they neither marry, nor are given in marriage, but are as the angels of God in heaven. But as touching the resurrection of the dead, have ye not read that which was spoken unto you by God, saying, I am the God of Abraham, and the God of Isaac, and the God of Jacob? God is not the God of the dead, but of the living" (Matt. 22:29-32).

2. Job 19:25-27. Most scholars believe that the book of Job reflects the patriarchal period and, therefore, is a very early book. Job asked the question, "If a man die, shall he live again?" (14:14). Later he reached this conclusion, "For I know that my redeemer liveth, and that he shall stand at the latter day upon the earth: and though after my skin worms destroy this body, yet in my flesh shall I see God: whom I shall see for myself, and mine eyes shall behold, and not another; though my reins be consumed within me" (19:25-27).

Job asked the question, "If a man die, shall he live again?"

For other Old Testament references that imply the resurrection, see the following: Psalm 16:8-11; 17:15; 49:15; 73:24; Isaiah 25:8; 26:19; Daniel 12:2; Hosea 13:14.

The Pharisee/Sadducee Conflict over Resurrection

The first century Sadducees denied the resurrection of the body (Matt. 22:23; Acts 23:8). In this respect they differed from the Pharisees. On one occasion they challenged Jesus with their "unanswerable" logic (Matt. 22:23-33). Jesus clearly demonstrated that he rejected the Sadducees' position on the resurrection by his use of Exodus 3:6 to affirm that God is the God of the living.

The Apostle Paul was a Pharisee before his conversion, indicating his rejection of the Sadducees' concept of the dead. After he became a Christian and was on trial before the Jewish authorities, he clearly identified himself with the Pharisees and against the Sadducees with reference to the resurrection of the dead. Acts 23:6-8 records,

> Then Paul, knowing that some of them were Sadducees and the others Pharisees, called out in the Sanhedrin, "My brothers, I am a Pharisee, the son of a Pharisee. I stand on trial because of my hope in the resurrection of the dead." When he said this, a dispute broke out between the Pharisees and the Sadducees, and the assembly was divided. (The Sadducees say that there is no resurrection, and that there are neither angels nor spirits, but the Pharisees acknowledge them all.)

The Scriptures are clear in showing that both Jesus and Paul rejected the Sadducees' denial of the resurrection and, with the Pharisees, affirmed belief in the resurrection.

The New Testament Teaches a Bodily Resurrection

The word "resurrection" in New Testament is frequently translated from *anastasis* which means "**1.** *a raising up, rising,* (e.g. fr. a seat)... **2.** *a rising from the dead"* (Thayer 42). It is used of the resurrection of Jesus from the dead (Acts 1:22; 2:31; 4:33; Rom 6:5; etc.) and the resurrection of all men at the end of the present age (Matt. 22:30, 31; Mark 12:18, 23; etc.). The soul does not die; hence, it is not that which shall be raised. The dead body is what shall be raised. The following verses clearly affirm the resurrection of the dead:

The soul does not die; hence, it is not that which shall be raised.

1. John 5:21, 25, 28-29. In his discussion with the Jews, Jesus affirmed his deity, making himself equal with God (5:17). Rather than saying the Jews misunderstood what he claimed for himself, Jesus more definitely affirmed his deity by saying that he had the power of life within himself, both the power to impart new spiritual life and to raise the dead. He said,

> For as the Father raiseth up the dead, and quickeneth them; even so the Son quickeneth whom he will.... Verily, verily, I say unto you, The hour is coming, and now is, when the dead shall hear the voice of the Son of God: and they that hear shall live.... Marvel not at this: for the hour is coming, in the which all that are in the graves shall hear his voice, and shall come forth; they that have done good, unto the resurrection of life; and they that have done evil, unto the resurrection of damnation (John 5:28-29).

2. Acts 4:1-2. The Sadducees took offence at the apostles' preaching in Jerusalem. The text records, "And as they spake unto the people, the priests, and the captain of the temple, and the Sadducees, came upon them, being grieved that they taught the people, and *preached through Jesus the resurrection from the dead."* Obviously, first century preaching included preaching the resurrection of the dead through Jesus.

3. 1 Corinthians. The most extensive discussion of the resurrection occurs in the books of 1-2 Corinthians. The reason for that may not be so obvious to those unacquainted with Grecian thought. In Grecian thought, the resurrection was not desired; what was desired was release from the body. These wrong beliefs were challenged and opposed by Paul.

1 Corinthians 6:14-15 says, "And God hath both raised up the Lord, and *will also raise up us* by his own power. Know ye not that your bodies are the members of Christ? Shall I then take the members of Christ, and make them the members of an harlot? God forbid." The Corinthians believed that the sinful body was unimportant. In contrast to that, Paul argues that the body will be raised from the dead and that our "bodies" are the members of Christ which should not be joined to a harlot. The body is the temple of the Holy Spirit (6:19). We are bought with a price and therefore should glorify God "in your body, and in your spirit, which are God's" (6:20). The body as well as the spirit belongs to God and God will raise it from the dead.

The most extensive discussion of the resurrection occurs in 1 Corinthians 15, the text of which is not reproduced here. The argument

NOTES

is not merely to affirm the resurrection of Christ from the dead, but to affirm the resurrection of the dead, using Christ's resurrection as the guarantee of our own resurrection. Here is the outline of the chapter:

a. *15:1-4.* The gospel which Paul originally preached included the affirmation of the death, burial, and resurrection of Christ. This is what they believed, received, and in which they stand.

b. *15:5-11.* The resurrection of Christ from the dead was confirmed by eyewitness testimony and is part and parcel of what all of the apostles preached. "Therefore whether it were I or they, so we preach, and so ye believed" (15:11).

c. *15:12-19.* The resurrection of Jesus proves that the dead are raised. How can one say there is no resurrection of the dead and believe in the resurrection of Jesus (15:12-13)? If the dead are not raised, then Christ was not raised (15:16). Paul then develops a series of arguments to demonstrate that the resurrection of Christ from the dead is central to the gospel message. If Christ is not raised, (1) our preaching is vain (15:14); (2) your faith is vain (15:14); (3) we are false witnesses of God (15:15); (4) you are yet in your sins (15:17); (5) those who have died have perished (18). Those who have hope in Christ only in this life are to be pitied (15:19).

d. *15:20-28.* This extensive argument is as follows: (a) Christ is the "first-fruits" of them that slept (15:20). The word "first-fruits" is from *aparchē* which is defined as follows: "Christ is called *ap. tōn kekoimēmenōn* as the first one recalled to life of them that have fallen asleep, 1 Co. xv.20, 23 (here the phrase seems to signify that by his case the future resurrection of Christians is guaranteed; because the first-fruits forerun and are, as it were, a pledge and promise of the rest of the harvest)" (Thayer, 54). (b) "For since by man came death, by man came also the resurrection of the dead. For as in Adam all die, even so in Christ shall all be made alive" (15:21-22). The word "all" is just as extensive in one part of 15:22 as in the other. "All" die in Adam and "all" are made alive in Christ. The sense in which "alive" is used in this verse is with reference to the resurrection. Jesus is the one who made possible the resurrection of all men (both the just and the unjust). (c) The resurrection will occur in its own order: first Christ, as the first-fruits, and afterward those who are his at his coming (15:23). This will occur at the "end" when Christ will "deliver up" the kingdom to the Father, when "he shall have put down all rule and all authority and power" (15:24-25). The last enemy that must be destroyed is "death" (15:26). When death is destroyed by the resurrection, then Christ will deliver up the kingdom to the Father and be subject to him who submitted all things under him (15:27-28).

e. *15:29-34.* This section argues the consequences of there being no resurrection of the dead. We were baptized on the belief that there is a resurrection from the dead (15:29). If there is no resurrection, there is no reason to risk one's life for the gospel (15:30-32). Paul warned the Corinthians of the danger to the soul that those who denied the resurrection had saying, "Be not deceived: evil communications corrupt good manners" (15:33). He exhorted those without a knowledge of the resurrection to "awake to righteousness" (15:34). Their denial of the resurrection was a shame to them.

f. *15:35-49.* This section answers objections to the resurrection. In 15:35-36, Paul answered the objection, "How are the dead raised up?" He compared the burial of the dead body to sowing a grain and the resurrection of the body to the sprouting of a new plant from the planted seed. In 15:37-49, he answers the argument "With what body do they come?" In response, Paul said,

NOTES

"But God giveth it a body as it hath pleased him" (15:38). He illustrated how God had given various bodies to every sort of his creation fitted for the environment in which they lived (15:38-41) and then affirmed that the resurrection body would be fitted for its eternal home (15:42). "It is sown in corruption; it is raised in incorruption: it is sown in dishonour; it is raised in glory: it is sown in weakness; it is raised in power: It is sown a natural body; it is raised a spiritual body. There is a natural body, and there is a spiritual body" (15:42-44). Just as certainly as there is a natural body, there will be a "spiritual body." This is guaranteed by the second Adam (15:45). The work of Christ is the means by which the resurrection of the body will occur (15:46-48). Paul concludes by affirming that we shall bear the image of the heavenly just as

. . . the prophetic purpose is not consummated until every man who is in the tomb is raised from the dead.

certainly as we have born the image of the earthly. The "image of the heavenly" which we shall bear is the resurrected body which Jesus himself had.

g. 15:50-53. This section promises that those who are alive when Jesus comes again will have their physical bodies changed into the same "spiritual body" as the raised will possess.

h. 15:54-57. The resurrection of the dead body and the change of the living bodies who are subject to death will bring to fulfillment the prophecies that foretold the defeat of death. In that sense, the prophetic purpose is not consummated until every man who is in the tomb is raised from the dead.

i. 15:58. Because of our assurance of the resurrection, we can live in certainty and hope, knowing that the works that we do for Christ in this body will not be lost by death.

4. 2 Corinthians 4:14-5:10. Paul described the fleshly body as "our earthly house of this tabernacle" which is dissolved by death (5:1). However, there will be "a building of God, an house not made with hands, eternal in the heavens" to house his spirit (5:1). In this fleshly body, he groaned looking for that eternal house (5:2). Being so clothed, "we shall not be found naked" (5:3).[1] Consequently, the Christian hope is, not to be found naked (without a body), but to be clothed with the resurrection body (5:4).

5. 1 Thessalonians 4:13-18. Paul wrote, But I would not have you to be ignorant, brethren, concerning them which are asleep, that ye sorrow not, even as others which have no hope. For if we believe that Jesus died and rose again, even so them also which sleep in Jesus will God bring with him. For this we say unto you by the word of the Lord, that we which are alive and remain unto the coming of the Lord shall not prevent them which are asleep. For the Lord himself shall descend from heaven with a shout, with the voice of the archangel, and with the trump of God: and the dead in Christ shall rise first: Then we which are alive and remain shall be caught up together with them in the clouds, to meet the Lord in the air: and so shall we ever be with the Lord. Wherefore comfort one another with these words.

This passage is very similar to the teaching of 1 Corinthians 15. This passage teaches that Jesus will bring the spirits of the righteous dead with him

[1] Being found naked is used to describe a bodiless spirit. The Christian hope is not of a bodiless spirit going to heaven to be with God. Rather, it is a spirit housed in resurrected body.

NOTES

and then "the dead" (bodies) shall rise first. Here the body and the spirit will be reunited before those who are living will be changed.

The Bible Teaches a General Resurrection

1. All shall be raised from the dead. "All" that are in the tomb shall come forth, some to a resurrection of life and some to a resurrection of condemnation. "Marvel not at this: for the hour is coming, in the which *all* that are in the graves shall hear his voice, and shall come forth; they that have done good, unto the resurrection of life; and they that have done evil, unto the resurrection of damnation" (John 5:28-29). Paul said the same thing as Jesus did, "But this I confess unto thee, that after the way which they call heresy, so worship I the God of my fathers, believing all things which are written in the law and in the prophets: and have hope toward God, which they themselves also allow, that there shall be a resurrection of the dead, both of the just and unjust" (Acts 24:14-15).

2. The resurrection will occur at the Lord's second coming which is the "last day." Jesus said,

> And this is the Father's will which hath sent me, that of all which he hath given me I should lose nothing, but should raise it up again *at the last day*. And this is the will of him that sent me, that every one which seeth the Son, and believeth on him, may have everlasting life: and I will raise him up *at the last day*.... No man can come to me, except the Father which hath sent me draw him: and I will raise him up *at the last day*.... Whoso eateth my flesh, and drinketh my blood, hath eternal life; and I will raise him up *at the last day* (John 6:39-40, 44, 54).

The authority of Scripture must be challenged to deny the resurrection, because Scripture so clearly affirms the resurrection.

The "last trumpet" ("the trumpet after which no other will sound," Thayer 253) will sound (1 Cor. 15:52) and the dead shall rise.

The dead shall be raised at "the hour" when those who are in the graves hear Jesus voice and come forth (John 5:28-29).

Conclusion

To deny that the body is going to be raised from the dead is to deny what the Scriptures clearly affirm will happen. The authority of Scripture must be challenged to deny the resurrection, because Scripture so clearly affirms the resurrection.

NOTES

Questions

1. How does Exodus 3:6 indicate the resurrection? ______________________________

2. What was Job's hope to explain his undeserved suffering (19:25-27)? ______________________________

3. Give the respective beliefs of the following regarding the resurrection of the dead (Acts 23:6-8):
   a. Sadducees: ______________________________
   b. Pharisees: ______________________________
   c. Paul: ______________________________
4. What is raised from the dead? ______________________________
5. Who will raise men from the dead (John 5:21, 25, 28-29)? ______________________________
6. Why did the Sadducees oppose apostolic preaching (Acts 4:1-2)? ______________________________

7. What was the Grecian expectation or hope for the body? ______________________________

8. What does 1 Corinthians 6:14-20 teach about the body's destiny? ______________________________

9. What does Christ being the "first fruits" of the resurrection mean (1 Cor. 15:20)? ______________________________

10. Who will be raised from the dead (1 Cor. 15:21-22)? ______________________________
11. How will death be destroyed (1 Cor. 15:26)? ______________________________
12. How is the resurrection compared to sowing grain (1 Cor. 15:35-36)? ______________________________

13. What does 1 Corinthians 15:37-49 teach about the nature of the resurrection body? ______________________________

14. What will happen to the living when Jesus returns and raises the dead (1 Cor. 15:50-53)? ______________________________

15. Who will be raised according to Acts 24:14-15? ______________________________
16. When will the resurrection occur (John 6:40, 44, 54)? ______________________________
17. How does John 5:28-29 show that the resurrection of the righteous and wicked will not be separated by a thousand years? ______________________________

Lesson 8

The Destruction of the Heavens and Earth

Many people think that when Jesus comes back to this earth, he will establish an earthly kingdom and reign on this earth for a thousand years. One of the things wrong with this theory is the fact that the earth and the works in it will be destroyed at the second coming of Christ.

Others believe that matter is eternal. These are those who do not believe in creation or a Creator. They also see no end to creation. They may believe that there is going to be some great cosmic explosion but they do not see the destruction of the heavens and the earth in the biblical sense.

Some believe that the earth will be rejuvenated and become heaven. There are no Bible verses that indicate that this is so.

The Bible Foretells the End of the World

Passages in both the Old and New Testaments speak of the destruction of the heavens and the earth. Consider them:

1. Job 14:12. "So man lieth down, and riseth not: *till the heavens be no more*, they shall not awake, nor be raised out of their sleep" (Job 14:12). Job spoke of a time when the heavens would be no more, during which time man's body would lie in the grave. He also foresaw a time when that body would be raised (19:25-26).

2. Psalm 102:25-26. "Of old hast thou laid the foundation of the earth: and the heavens are the work of thy hands. *They shall perish*, but thou shalt endure: yea, all of them shall wax old like a garment; as a vesture shalt thou change them, and they shall be changed." In contrast to the eternal, unchanging God, the psalmist recognized that the created world "shall perish."

3. Isaiah 34:4. "And all the host of heaven *shall be dissolved*, and the heavens shall be rolled together as a scroll: and all their host shall fall down, as the leaf falleth off from the vine, and as a falling fig from the fig tree." In the context of Isaiah's description of God's final judgment, Isaiah prophesied of the destruction of the heavens and earth. This chapter also speaks of the everlasting punishment of the wicked (34:10).

4. Isaiah 51:6. "Lift up your eyes to the heavens, and look upon the earth beneath: for *the heavens shall vanish away like smoke*, and the earth shall wax old like a garment, and they that dwell therein shall die in like manner: but my salvation shall be for ever, and my righteousness shall not be abolished." To contrast God's everlasting salvation with things temporal, Isaiah said that it would outlast the physical creation.

5. Jesus' sermon prophesying the destruction of Jerusalem. In all three accounts of this sermon, Jesus said, "Heaven and earth shall pass away, but my words shall not pass away" (Matt. 24:35; cf. Mark 13:31; Luke 21:33). Jesus plainly announced that heaven and earth would pass away. In contrast, his everlasting word will never be destroyed.

6. 1 John 2:17. "And the world passeth away, and the lust thereof: but he that doeth the will of God abideth for ever." One of the reasons Christians are exhorted not to love the world is because it will pass away.

. . . the physical world which was created by God and used by him to his glory, will also be destroyed by him when its purpose is over.

7. Revelation 20:11. "And I saw a great white throne, and him that sat on it, from whose face the earth and the heaven fled away; and there was found no place for them." The same thought is repeated in Revelation 21:1, "And I saw a new heaven and a new earth: for the first heaven and the first earth were passed away; and there was no more sea." The earth and heavens will have passed away when God establishes his new heavens and new earth (heaven).

These verses emphasize to us that the physical world which was created by God and used by him to his glory, will also be destroyed by him when its purpose is over.

The Destruction of the Heavens and Earth Will Occur At Christ's Second Coming

The most extensive prophecy of the destruction of the heavens and earth occurs in 2 Peter 3. In answer to mockers who denied the Lord's second coming, Peter reminded them that the Lord had previously destroyed this world with water during the flood (3:5-6). This heaven and earth are kept in store by the same word "reserved unto fire against the day of the judgment and perdition of ungodly men" (3:7). He then describes the Lord's second coming saying, "But the day of the Lord will come as a thief in the night; in the which the heavens shall pass away with a great noise, and the elements shall melt with fervent heat, the earth also and the works that are therein shall be burned up" (2 Pet. 3:10). He concludes by exhorting, "Seeing then that all these things shall be dissolved, what manner of persons ought ye to be in all holy conversation and godliness, looking for and hasting unto the coming of the day of God, wherein the heavens being on fire shall be dissolved, and the elements shall melt with fervent heat?" (2 Pet. 3:11-12).

The heavens and earth will be destroyed when the "day of the Lord" comes like a "thief in the night." We know what will occur: the heavens and earth will be destroyed. We know when it will occur: when the Lord comes again.

One of the reasons that we will have to have a changed body to dwell in heaven is because of the new world in which we will live (1 Cor. 15:51-58). Our physical bodies are suited to this world, but will not be suited for the world to come. Consequently, the physical body will be changed and clothed in a body suited to the place in which we dwell.

NOTES

Questions

1. In the passages cited below, quote the portion that states that the world will be destroyed:
   a. Job 14:12: ______
   b. Psalm 102:25-26: ______
   c. Isaiah 34:4: ______
   d. Isaiah 51:6: ______
   e. Matthew 24:35 (cf. Mark 13:31; Luke 21:33): ______
   f. 1 John 2:17: ______
   g. Revelation 20:11: ______
   h. Revelation 21:1: ______
2. From a study of 2 Peter 3, answer these questions:
   a. What were scoffers of the first century saying (3:3-4)? ______
   b. What Old Testament proof showed that the world had not always operated as it presently is (3:5-6)?
   ______
   ______
   c. What is the world that will be destroyed (3:7)? ______
   d. What is reserved for the world (3:7)? ______
   e. When will that occur (3:7)? ______
   f. Why is God delaying this judgment (3:8-9)? ______
   g. In what way is the day of the Lord coming like a thief (3:10)? ______
   h. What will happen to the world when he comes again (3:10)? ______
   i. What does 3:11 say will happen to the world? ______
   j. What does 3:12 say will happen to the world? ______

Lesson 9

The Judgment

Following the Lord's second coming and the resurrection of the dead, the final judgment will occur. This judgment must be distinguished from God's temporal judgments against nations (the Flood, destruction of Babylon, destruction of Jerusalem in A.D. 70; etc.). Numerous passages speak of the final judgment, such as the following:

> But I say unto you, That it shall be more tolerable for the land of Sodom in the day of judgment, than for thee (Matt. 11:24).

> And as he reasoned of righteousness, temperance, and judgment to come, Felix trembled, and answered, Go thy way for this time; when I have a convenient season, I will call for thee (Acts 24:25).

> And as it is appointed unto men once to die, but after this the judgment (Heb. 9:27).

This lesson is designed to study the final judgment.

The Necessity of the Judgment

If justice and righteousness exist, there must be a final judgment. This world is full of many inequities. Many men, such as Stephen, did not receive justice in their lifetimes (Acts 7). Wicked men get away with every kind of crime, if one is only considering the temporal punishment of sin. Seeing the wicked prosper has long been a problem for man (Psa. 73). Malachi recorded the reasoning of Israelites of his day when he wrote, "Ye have said, It is vain to serve God: and what profit is it that we have kept his ordinance, and that we have walked mournfully before the Lord of hosts? And now we call the proud happy; yea, they that work wickedness are set up; yea, they that tempt God are even delivered" (Mal. 3:14-15).

We live in an imperfect world in which the wicked are not always punished for their crimes and sometimes the righteous suffer (e.g., the crucifixion of Jesus, the persecution of saints, the holocaust, etc.). If there is to be any justice, there must be a final judgment. Otherwise, wickedness sometimes does pay.

When Will the Final Judgment Occur?

The Bible states that the final judgment of man will occur after the second coming of the Lord Jesus. In the Parable of the Tares (Matt. 13:24-30, 36-43), Jesus foretold the final separation of the wicked from the righteous and told us when that would occur: "As therefore the tares are gathered and burned in the fire; so shall it be *in the end of this world*" (Matt. 13:40). In the Parable of the Separation of the Sheep and Goats (Matt. 25:31-46), Jesus told when judgment will occur, "*When the Son of man shall come in his glory*, and all the holy angels with him, then shall he sit upon the throne of his glory: And before him shall be gathered all nations: and he shall separate them one from another, as a shepherd divideth his sheep from the goats" (Matt. 25:31-32).

Paul told the events that would happen when Jesus comes again:

> And to you who are troubled rest with us, when the Lord Jesus shall be revealed from heaven with his mighty angels, in flaming fire taking vengeance

> on them that know not God, and that obey not the gospel of our Lord Jesus Christ: who shall be punished with everlasting destruction from the presence of the Lord, and from the glory of his power; when he shall come to be glorified in his saints, and to be admired in all them that believe (because our testimony among you was believed) in that day (2 Thess. 1:7-10).

The punishing of the wicked and the glorifying of the righteous presupposes a separation of the two groups, hence a judgment.

Peter foretold that the world is reserved for a judgment ("But the heavens and the earth, which are now, by the same word are kept in store, reserved unto fire against the day of judgment and perdition of ungodly men," 2 Pet.3:7), that will occur when Jesus comes back and destroys this world with fire (2 Pet. 3:9-14).

The book of Revelation pictures this great judgment: "And I saw the dead, small and great, stand before God; and the books were opened: and another book was opened, which is the book of life: and the dead were judged out of those things which were written in the books, according to their works" (Rev. 20:12). This judgment occurred after the heaven and earth are "fled away" (Rev. 20:11). Consequently, we conclude that God's final judgment shall occur at the second coming of Jesus, after the dead have been raise and the heaven and earth have been destroyed.

The Judge

We can be thankful that some who pass judgment on Christians in this world will not be the ones who pass final judgment. The world will not be our judge. The standards by which the world judges are not the same as the Lord uses. Therefore, the world condemns Christians for doing some things which the Lord commend us for doing (for example, condemnation of abortion and homosexuality; preaching the oneness of the church). The brethren will not be our judges. In past ages the majority of brethren condemned those who opposed the introduction of instrumental music in worship and church support of human institutions. Fortunately, these brethren will not be our judges. My family will not be my judge. Some families break off association with those who become Christians; some families defend their members even when they practice sin. My own conscience will not be my judge in the day of final judgment.

The Scriptures clearly teach that judgment belongs to Jehovah. Consider these passages:

> But without faith it is impossible to please him: for he that cometh to God must believe that he is, and that he is a rewarder of them that diligently seek him (Heb. 11:6).
>
> And if ye call on the Father, who without respect of persons judgeth according to every man's work, pass the time of your sojourning here in fear (1 Pet. 1:17).
>
> Who, when he was reviled, reviled not again; when he suffered, he threatened not; but committed himself to him that judgeth righteously (1 Pet. 2:23).

The Lord's righteous judgment will be administered by his Son, as the following passages show:

> When the Son of man shall come in his glory, and all the holy angels with him, then shall he sit upon the throne of his glory: And before him shall be gathered all nations: and he shall separate them one from another, as a shepherd divideth his sheep from the goats (Matt. 25:31-32).
>
> For the Father judgeth no man, but hath committed all judgment unto the Son:... And hath given him authority to execute judgment also, because he is the Son of man (John 5:22, 27).

NOTES

> And he commanded us to preach unto the people, and to testify that it is he which was ordained of God to be the Judge of quick and dead (Acts 10:42).

> And the times of this ignorance God winked at; but now commandeth all men every where to repent: Because he hath appointed a day, in the which he will judge the world in righteousness by that man whom he hath ordained; whereof he hath given assurance unto all men, in that he hath raised him from the dead (Acts 17:30-31).

> For we must all appear before the judgment seat of Christ; that every one may receive the things done in his body, according to that he hath done, whether it be good or bad (2 Cor. 5:10).

> I charge thee therefore before God, and the Lord Jesus Christ, who shall judge the quick and the dead at his appearing and his kingdom (2 Tim. 4:1).

> Henceforth there is laid up for me a crown of righteousness, which the Lord, the righteous judge, shall give me at that day: and not to me only, but unto all them also that love his appearing (2 Tim. 4:8).

Jesus will be assisted in his judgment by angels (Matt. 13:41-43; 24:31; 25:31).[1]

The Qualifications of the Judge

Jesus is the best qualified to judge man. What qualifications must our judge have? Even as we think about the qualifications for Supreme Court justices, think about the qualifications of the judge at the end of time.

1. He must be deity. No one who is not deity is qualified to judge. Paul said, "Therefore judge nothing before the time, until the Lord come, who both will bring to light the hidden things of darkness, and will make manifest the counsels of the hearts: and then shall every man have praise of God" (1 Cor. 4:5). A judge must be qualified to know the things hidden from man's sight—all the pertinent facts, all of the circumstances that might contribute to a situation, the man's intentions, etc. Only God can know these things for certain.

Jesus is the best qualified to judge man. No one who is not deity is qualified to judge... a qualified judge must understand man's condition and circumstance. Who is better able to know that than one who has experienced the human condition?

2. He must understand the human condition. On the other hand, a qualified judge must understand man's condition and circumstance. Who is better able to know that than one who has experienced the human condition? He was himself tempted and knows what our conflict with sin is (Heb. 2:17-18; 4:15).

3. He must be impartial. The final judgment will be a righteous judgment (Acts 17:30-31). It must, therefore, be administered without respect of persons (Rom. 2:11).

The Standard of Judgment

There are some standards of judgment that will not be the standard used in divine judgment, such as: (a) The world's judgments of what is

[1] 1 Corinthians 6:2-3 says, "Do ye not know that the saints shall judge the world? And if the world shall be judged by you, are ye unworthy to judge the smallest matters? Know ye not that we shall judge angels? How much more things that pertain to this life?" This passage speaks of saints assisting in Christ's judgment. How those who will be judged will also judge is unclear, so I will only quote this passage and call it to your attention.

NOTES

right and wrong; (b) One's conscience; (c) What brethren think of a person. Paul said, "But with me it is a very small thing that I should be judged of you, or of man's judgment: yea, I judge not mine own self. For I know nothing by myself; yet am I not hereby justified: but he that judgeth me is the Lord" (1 Cor. 4:3-4). Rather, the standard to be used in judgment will be the revealed word of God. Jesus said, "He that rejecteth me, and receiveth not my words, hath one that judgeth him: *the word that I have spoken, the same shall judge him in the last day*" (John 12:48). Those who lived during the ages prior to the coming of Christ will be judged on the revelation given to them (Luke 16:31; Rom. 2:1-16). However, all men, whether Christians or non-Christians, will be held accountable to the revelation God has given through Christ (Acts 17:30-31).

Who Will Be Judged?

The judgment will involve every man who has ever lived (Matt. 25:32; Rom. 2:5-6; 3:6; Rev. 20:12-13). It will also include a judgment of angels (2 Pet. 2:4; Jude 6).

What Will Be Judged?

The Lord's judgment will involve men's (a) deeds (2 Cor. 5:10; Matt. 25:35-40; Rev. 20:12; Eph. 6:8; Heb. 6:10); (b) words (Matt. 12:36); and (c) thoughts (1 Cor. 4:5; Heb. 4:12-13). All will be exposed when the Lord's righteous judgment occurs (Luke 12:2-3; Matt. 6:4, 6, 18; 1 Tim. 5:24-25).

The Purpose of the Judgment

1. It is not investigative. Human tribunals assemble to consider the evidence of whether a person is guilty or innocent of a given crime. Evidence and counter evidence are presented by the prosecutor and defense. The Lord's judgment is not investigative inasmuch as the Omniscient God already knows all things; he knows who is guilty and who is innocent. Furthermore, he has already demonstrated with reference to those who died before the second coming what the eternal destiny of each is by whether the individual was sent to Abraham's bosom or torment.

The Lord's judgment is not investigative inasmuch as the Omniscient God already knows all things; he knows who is guilty and who is innocent.

2. The judgment will declare the glory of God. L. Berkhof wrote, "It will serve the purpose rather of displaying before all rational creatures the declarative glory of God in a formal, forensic act, which magnifies on the one hand His holiness and righteousness, and on the other hand, His grace and mercy" (*Systematic Theology,* 731).

3. The judgment will convict the ungodly. Jude wrote, "And Enoch also, the seventh from Adam, prophesied of these, saying, Behold, the Lord cometh with ten thousands of his saints, to execute judgment upon all, and to convince all that are ungodly among them of all their ungodly deeds which they have ungodly committed, and of all their hard speeches which ungodly sinners have spoken against him" (Jude 14-15). If anyone thinks he is not deserving of eternal torment, he will be convicted of his sins at judgment.

4. The judgment will execute God's judgment. The sentence will be passed and then carried out. Judgment will be executed.

NOTES

Questions

1. List several temporal judgments that God has executed. ______

2. Cite two current examples of men escaping the just punishment for sin. ______

3. How does this show the need for a divine judgment day? ______

4. What solution did Asaph find for understanding the prosperity of the wicked (Psa. 73)? ______

5. What made the people of Malachi's day think it was vain to serve God (Mal. 3:14-15)? ______

6. When will the final judgment occur according to:
   a. Matt. 13:24-30, 36-43? ______
   b. Matt. 25:31-46? ______
   c. 2 Thess. 1:7-10? ______
   d. 2 Pet. 3:8-14? ______
   e. Rev. 20:11-14? ______

7. Why is Jesus the best qualified to judge men? ______

8. What proof does one have that Jesus truly will judge men (Acts 17:30-31)? ______

9. Why should we be glad that we are not judged by the following standards (1 Cor. 4:3-4): ______
   a. What the world thinks? ______
   b. What brethren think? ______
   c. One's conscience? ______

10. What standard will be used for judgment (John 12:48)? ______

11. Must one agree to be judged by that standard before it will be used? ______

12. Who will be judged? ____________________

13. What will be judged? ____________________

14. What is the purpose of the judgment? ____________________

Lesson 10

Hell: Eternal Damnation

Americans have generally moved away from belief in hell. Even Evangelical preachers are able to preach into heaven about anyone. John Gertsner wrote, "Even approximately twenty percent of evangelicals think they can be evangelical and live in disobedience to Christ" (*Repent or Perish,* 12). There are virtually no sermons being preached on hell. Some have become persuaded that the concept of a God who would send anyone to hell is contrary to their view of God. We have made "God-fearing" a bad word and concept (Acts 10:2, 35; 13:16).

We need to restore the biblical concept of the "terror of the Lord." Consider what the following texts state about man's need to fear the Lord.

> Knowing therefore the terror of the Lord, we persuade men; but we are made manifest unto God; and I trust also are made manifest in your consciences (2 Cor. 5:11).

> And fear not them which kill the body, but are not able to kill the soul: but rather fear him which is able to destroy both soul and body in hell (Matt. 10:28).

> Ye serpents, ye generation of vipers, how can ye escape the damnation of hell? (Matt. 23:33).

The terror of the Lord is what usually brings men to the foot of the cross of Christ. Until men realize their soul's danger and jeopardy, they seek no solution to it.

In this lesson, we propose to consider what the Bible teaches us about hell.

The Words Translated Hell

Sheol is the only Old Testament word translated "hell." Brown, Driver, and Briggs define the word to mean "the underworld. . . whither men descend at death" (see Ps. 16:10; 18:4, 5). They add that the conditions of the righteous and wicked are sometimes distinguished in *sheol. Sheol* for the wicked (see Ps. 9:17; 55:15) is: (a) A place of sorrows (2 Sam. 22:6); (b) A place of destruction (Prov. 15:11; 27:20); (c) The opposite of life (Prov. 15:24); (d) The pit (Isa. 14:15). It has depths (Prov. 9:18). These things are said about *sheol* for the righteous: (a) He shall not be abandoned there (Ps. 16:10); (b) God shall redeem him from there (Ps. 49:15).

In the King James Version, *hades* is translated "hell" in the New Testament. The Old Testament usage of *sheol* corresponds with the use of *hades* in the New Testament. In the LXX translation, *sheol* is almost always rendered by this word. It becomes the common receptacle of disembodied spirits (Thayer 11). (See Luke 16:23; Acts 2:27, 31.) The story of the rich man and Lazarus demonstrates that the "realm of the dead" has two compartments: Abraham's bosom (or Paradise, Luke 23:43) and torment. We need to understand that the dwellings of the righteous and the wicked are distinguished in *hades*.

Gehenna is the New Testament term that is generally used to refer to the place of everlasting punishment. The word was originally used to refer to the "Valley of Hinnom" south and east of Jerusalem. It began to be called *ben hinnom*, the valley of the sons of lamentation (from the Hebrew *naham*, to lament), so called because there the cries of the little children who were thrown into the fiery arms of the pagan god Moloch were heard (Thayer, 111). "The Jews so abhorred the place after these horrible sacrifices had been abolished by king Josiah (2 K. xxiij. 10), that they cast into it not only all manner of refuse, but even the dead bodies of animals and of unburied criminals who had been executed. And since fires were always needed to consume the dead bodies, that the air might not become tainted by the putrefaction, it came to pass that the place was called *geenna tou puros* (gehenna of fire, mw) . . . . then this name was transferred to that place in Hades where the wicked after death will suffer punishment" (Thayer, 111).

None of us can speak of hell except as it is revealed to us in the Bible. No one has been there and come back (despite the comments of those with near-death experiences). We can only learn of this place through revelation, through what God had told us.

Tartaros is used in 2 Peter 2:4. It is "the name of a subterranean region, doleful and dark, regarded by the ancient Greeks as the abode of the wicked dead, where they suffer punishment for their evil deeds; it answers to Gehenna of the Jews" (Thayer, 615).

What Hell Is Like

The following Old Testament allusions to hell help us understand what it is like:

- The punishment of Sodom and Gomorrah was a foretaste of hell (Gen. 19:24; Jude 7).
- Psalm 73:18-19—the wicked are cast down to destruction where they are consumed with terrors.
- Isaiah 33:14—sinners in Zion will receive everlasting burnings.
- Isaiah 34:8-10—the day of the Lord's vengeance shall bring everlasting burning.
- Isaiah 57:21—there is no peace for the wicked.
- Isaiah 66:24—the wicked will go to a place where their worm does not die and their fire is not quenched.
- Daniel 12:1-2,10—the wicked will awake to everlasting contempt.

None of us can speak of hell except as it is revealed to us in the Bible. No one has been there and come back (despite the comments of those with near-death experiences). We can only learn of this place through revelation, through what God had told us. Jesus told us more about hell than any other person (only one New Testament usage of gehenna was not spoken by Jesus, see James 3:6). Here is how he described hell:

- Matthew 5:22—hell fire.

NOTES

- Matthew 5:29-30; 18:9—better to lose hand, foot, or eye in this life than to go there.
- Matthew 10:28—a place where God can destroy both body and soul.
- Matthew 13:41-42—a furnace of fire where there will be weeping and gnashing of teeth.
- Matthew 23:33—a place of damnation.
- Matthew 25:30—a place of outer darkness where there is weeping and gnashing of teeth.
- Matthew 25:41—a place of everlasting fire prepared for the devil and his angels.
- Matthew 25:46—a place of everlasting punishment.
- Mark 9:43-48—a place where the fire is not quenched and the worm does not die.

Other passages speak of the damnation of hell without using the word *gehenna*. Here are some of those passages and how they describe eternal torment:

- Matthew 8:10-12—outer darkness where there is weeping and gnashing of teeth.
- Matthew 8:29—the evil spirits recognize that there is a time for torment.
- Luke 13:3—those who do not repent will perish.
- Luke 13:22-30—the workers of iniquity will be forced to "depart" from the presence of the Lord.
- Luke 16:19-31—the story of the rich man and Lazarus teaches everlasting torment.
- John 3:16, 36—unbelievers shall be condemned.
- John 5:28-29—some will be raised to receive damnation.
- Romans 2:5, 8-9—the Lord's wrath brings tribulation and anguish.
- Romans 2:12—to perish.
- Romans 5:9—God's wrath.
- 2 Thessalonians 1:7-9—the vengeance of God punishes with everlasting destruction away from the presence of the Lord. As heaven is described as fellowship with God, torment is banishment from his presence.

Scare Tactics

Men belittle "hell fire and brimstone" preaching because it tends to scare people into obeying the gospel. Yet, Paul wrote, "Knowing therefore the terror of the Lord, we persuade men; but we are made manifest unto God; and I trust also are made manifest in your consciences" (2 Cor. 5:11). The truth is that men are not opposed to "scare tactics" as a means of motivation. They scare children away from fire, from electric sockets, from poisonous drinks or pills, from snakes, from certain toys, from anything that threatens them. Why should one be ashamed to scare people about the dangers of hell?

One cannot be scared into heaven, but he may be so afraid of hell that he turns to Christ as the means of escape from this torment. Very few people who will go to heaven ever obey the gospel to be saved unless they first realize their lost condition outside of Christ and recognize that being lost means going to everlasting hell.

NOTES

- Hebrews 10:28-31—a punishment worse than death without mercy, the vengeance of the living God.
- 2 Peter 2:17—eternal mist of darkness.
- Jude 7, 13—the vengeance of eternal fire, the blackness of darkness.
- Revelation 14:10-11—the torment of fire and brimstone, no rest night and day forever.
- Revelation 21:8—the lake that burns with fire and brimstone.

How Long Will the Punishment Last?

The Lord who spoke to us about hell described hell's duration as follows:

- The place prepared for the devils and his angels (Matt. 25:41); already the angels have been held in the bondage of torment for thousands of years (2 Pet. 2:4; Jude 6). They will be tormented day and night forever and ever (Rev. 20:10).
- A place of everlasting fire (Matt. 18:8; 25:46). Hell lasts just as long as heaven does (Matt. 25:41); the vengeance of an eternal fire (Jude 7).
- The smoke of their torment ascends up forever (Rev. 14:10-11).
- God's wrath abides on him (John 3:36).
- A place where the worm does not die and the fire is not quenched (Mark 9:44, 46, 48).
- Everlasting destruction from the presence of God (2 Thess. 1:6-9).
- The blackness of darkness forever (2 Pet. 2:17; Jude 12-13).

Hell is an eternal punishment, a place from which there is no escape.

Who Will Go There?

Here is what the Bible tells us about who will be in hell:

- The devil and his angels will go to *gehenna* (Matt. 25:41), but they have already been held in chains of darkness because of their sins (2 Pet. 2:4).
- Some religious people (Matt. 7:13-14).
- Those who do not obey the Lord (2 Thess. 1:7-9).
- The ungodly and immoral (Rev. 21:8; 22:5; Gal. 5:19-21; 1 Cor. 6:9-11).
- Lukewarm members (Rev. 3:15-16).
- The uncharitable (Matt. 25:31-46).
- Those whose names are not written in the book of life (Rev. 20:15).

Why Is Hell Necessary?

Hell is necessary for there to be justice. Many escape temporal consequences for their sins. The righteous have frequently fretted that the wicked prosper (Job 21:7; Pss. 37:1-2; 73; Prov. 3:31; 24:1). Even Jesus foretold that righteous men would suffer (Matt. 5:10-12; 1 Pet. 4:16). If this world is the only place for justice, then there is no absolute justice. Hell demonstrates the justice of a righteous God. There the wicked will be punished. There will be no escaping from his righteous judgment. Position, power, wealth, and other things that are sometimes used on earth to escape the punishment for one's sins cannot thwart God's final judgment.

NOTES

Questions

1. Why should men fear God (2 Cor. 5:11)? ______________________________

   ____

2. How is the fear of God related to obedience? ______________________________

   ____

3. Define the following terms:

   a. Sheol: ______________________________

   b. Hades: ______________________________

   c. Gehenna: ______________________________

   d. Tartaros: ______________________________

4. What do the following Old Testament texts reveal about the nature of eternal torment:

   a. Genesis 19:24 (cf. Jude 7): ______________________________

   b. Psalm 73:18-19: ______________________________

   c. Isaiah 33:14: ______________________________

   d. Isaiah 34:8-10: ______________________________

   e. Isaiah 57:21: ______________________________

   f. Isaiah 66:24: ______________________________

   g. Daniel 12:1-2, 10: ______________________________

5. What did Jesus say about hell in the following passages?

   a. Matthew 5:22: ______________________________

   b. Matthew 5:29, 30; 18:9: ______________________________

   c. Matthew 8:10-12: ______________________________

   d. Matthew 10:28: ______________________________

   e. Matthew 13:41-42: ______________________________

   f. Matthew 23:33: ______________________________

   g. Matthew 25:30: ______________________________

   h. Matthew 25:41: ______________________________

   i. Matthew 25:46: ______________________________

j. Mark 9:43-46: ______

k. Luke 13:3: ______

l. Luke 16:19-31: ______

m. John 3:16: ______

6. What did the following New Testament texts say about the punishment of the wicked:

a. Romans 2:5, 8-9, 12: ______

b. 2 Thessalonians 1:7-9: ______

c. Hebrews 10:28-31: ______

d. Jude 7, 13: ______

e. Revelation 14:10-11; 21:8: ______

7. Who will be in hell? ______

______

8. What does the Bible teach about the duration of the punishment of hell? ______

______

9. Why is hell necessary? ______

______

Lesson 11

Heaven: The Reward of the Faithful

The eternal destiny of the righteous is called "heaven." The word heaven is used in several senses:

- The atmosphere, as opposed to the earth (see Heb. 1:10; 2 Pet. 3:5,10,12). This is the heavens in which the birds fly. The phrase "the heavens and the earth" is the equivalent to what we mean by the "universe."
- The starry heavens (see Heb. 11:12; Deut. 1:10; 10:22; etc.). This refers to outer space, the place of the sun, moon, stars, planets, and galaxies.
- The abode of God: the seat of the order of things eternal and consummately perfect, where God dwells and other heavenly beings. God is described as the "God of heaven" (2 Chron. 36:23; Neh. 1:4-5) and heaven is described as the abode of God (Isa. 57:15; 63:15; Matt. 6:9-10).

When we speak of "heaven" as the "reward of the faithful," we are speaking of the righteous being granted the privilege of dwelling eternally in the abode of God.

Who Will Be in Heaven?

The occupants of heaven are revealed to us as follows:

1. The Triune God. God the Father, God the Son, and God the Holy Spirit are in heaven (2 Chron. 36:23). The Son descended from heaven and returned there (John 3:13, 31; 6:33, 38, 42, 51, 58) and the Holy Spirit also descended from heaven (John 1:32). When saints go to heaven they go to be with God. John wrote, "And I heard a great voice out of heaven saying, Behold, the tabernacle of God is with men, and he will dwell with them, and they shall be his people, and God himself shall be with them, and be their God" (Rev. 21:3). What a tremendous blessing saints will receive to be in the presence of God throughout eternity. No one has seen the face of God (John 1:18), but in heaven God will dwell among us.

2. The Angels. The Scriptures speak of angels dwelling with God in heaven. These are ministering servants who do God's will (Matt. 18:10; 22:30; 24:36; etc.). What other spiritual beings exist in heaven is not fully known, although Revelation speaks of others (Rev. 4:4, 6; 5:6).

3. The Saved. Heaven is the future abode of the resurrected saints. (This should be distinguished from "Abraham's bosom" [Luke 16:22] or "Paradise" [Luke 23:43], as the abode of the saved, disembodied spirits. Heaven is prepared for the saved ones where they will dwell in their resurrected bodies.) Our salvation is laid up for us in heaven (Col. 1:5; 1 Pet. 1:4). Our names are written in heaven (Luke 10:20). We have a building of God in heaven (2 Cor. 5:1). Our reward is in heaven (Matt. 5:12). Our treasures are in heaven (Matt. 6:20; 19:21).

Those excluded from heaven are those who die in their sins. John wrote, "But the fearful, and unbelieving, and the abominable, and murderers, and whoremongers, and sorcerers, and idolaters, and all liars, shall have their part in the lake which burneth with fire and brimstone: which is the second death.... And there shall in no wise enter into it any thing that defileth, neither whatsoever worketh abomination, or maketh a lie: but they which are written in the Lamb's book of life" (Rev. 21:8, 27).

Men think about dwelling in neighborhoods that are safe. No one wants to dwell in a community where he must put bars on the windows to keep out criminals. Heaven will be a place of perfect peace and safety because there will be no sin there.

Heaven Holds All to Me

Earth holds no treasures but perish with using,
However precious they be;
Yet there's a country to which I am going,
Heaven holds all to me.

Out on the hills of that wonderful country,
Happy, contented and free,
Angels are waiting and watching my coming,
Heaven holds all to me.

Why should I long for the world and its sorrows,
When in that home o're the sea
Millions are singing the wonderful story?
Heaven holds all to me.

Heaven holds all to me,
Brighter its glory will be;
Joy without measure will be my treasure
Heaven holds all to be.

Tillit S. Teddlie

What Is Heaven Like?

Both heaven and hell are described in terms that men can understand. Undoubtedly metaphors and similes are used in describing our place of eternal bliss. Here are some figures used to describe heaven:

- Participation in the wedding feast (Matt. 22:1-14; 25:10). The church is described as the bride of Christ (Eph. 5:22-33). In the Jewish weddings of the first century, after the betrothal the groom went away until an appointed time when he came to take his bride home with him. When he returned with his bride a great marriage feast was celebrated. This picture is used of heaven in the passages cited above.
- The joys of the Lord (Matt. 25:21, 23). We can read of the "sorrows of our Lord" in the time of his betrayal, arrest, crucifixion and death. Heaven will be the "joys of our Lord" and he has invited us to share in them.
- Inheriting the Lord's kingdom (Matt. 25:34; cf. Acts 20:32; Eph. 1:11, 14; 1 Pet. 1:4-5). The concept of inheriting carries the idea of possessing. The kingdom of God is our permanent possession. Kingdoms of men pass away, but the kingdom of heaven will endure forever and the sovereign Lord will reign forever.
- Everlasting life (Matt. 25:46; cf. 7:14; 19:29). Spiritual life is the opposite of spiritual death, specifically, the second death. When we speak of being "dead" in sin, we speak of one who is separated from his God, because death is separation. Being alive unto God carries the idea of being in the fellowship of one's Lord. "Everlasting" describes the duration of this

NOTES

spiritual life in which one is unalienated from God.

- Sitting with Abraham, Isaac, and Jacob (Matt. 8:11), to be in the bosom of Abraham (Luke 16:23). The Bible presents the kingdom of heaven in terms of a great Messianic banquet where we have table fellowship with the Lord. The secular privilege of being invited to the king's table is the background for this figure of speech.
- To have Christ confess him before the Father (Matt. 10:32). Again, we think of the court of a king in which the son confesses his friendship with someone whom the king quickly welcomes as an honored guest. The Son of God will confess his association and friendship with those who are his children.
- To be ruler over all that the Lord has (Luke 12:43-44); ruling over cities (Luke 19:17, 19). In earthly kingdoms, the king appointed subordinates to oversee portions of his kingdom. Such subordinates enjoyed privileges not available to the common man. The figure is used to show the favored position of the child of God over the rest of mankind.
- Everlasting habitations (Luke 16:9). Our bodies are described as a "tabernacle," an earthly tent (2 Cor. 5:1). In contrast to this temporary dwelling place on an earth which will be destroyed by fire, the Christian will have a building not made with hands (an incorruptible body) that will dwell in everlasting habitations.

John saw heaven as a "new Jerusalem," a picture that was vivid in the mind of any Jewish Christian. The holy city, the new Jerusalem, came down out of heaven like a bride adorned for her husband (Rev. 21:2), a city prepared for those who are its inhabitants.

- A reward (Matt. 5:12; 10:42; 1 Cor. 3:14; Col. 2:18; 3:24; Heb. 11:26; etc.). The Greek word *misthos* conveys the idea "of the rewards which God bestows, or will bestow, upon good deeds and endeavors." This is not to be confused with earning wages, inasmuch as this would convey the idea of salvation by works. Rather, it is rewarding graciously those who have served God from great love.
- A home (Eccl. 12:5). The picture of home is one of the most beautiful pictures in human language. The warm home fellowship of father, mother, and siblings is the warmest association on earth. Home is the place where one dwells with God, his elder brother Jesus Christ, and all of the saved throughout eternity in the sweetest fellowship known.
- A reunion (1 Thess. 4:13-18; Matt. 8:11). The word "reunion" describes the renewal of association when family members who have been separated from one another over an

NOTES

extended period of time are able to have their association renewed. In heaven our association with saints who have gone before will be renewed. Many of our loved ones precede us in death. In the moment of our sorrow over their passing, this concept about heaven is so comforting.

- New Jerusalem (Rev. 3:12; 21:2, 10). Old Jerusalem was the religious capital of the state of Israel and the religious capital for the worship of God. Heaven is described as the new Jerusalem. It is the home of the king of the kingdom, the spiritual capital of the kingdom, and the place of endless worship.
- The Holy City (Rev. 21:2; 22:19). Parallel to the description of heaven as the "new Jerusalem" is the designation of it as the "holy city." It is the place where spiritual sacrifices are offered.
- A place where there is no night (Rev. 21:25; 22:5). Night is not merely the opposite of day light. Rather, the word is used in a spiritual sense to refer to spiritual darkness. The statement that there is no night in heaven emphasizes that this is a place without the presence of any sin (Rev. 21:8, 27).
- A place without the pains of earth life (Rev. 21:4). Suffering came to this world because of sin. Heaven, where there is no sin, is purged of those things on earth that make life miserable: sickness, death, distress, straits, turmoils, conflicts, etc. Heaven will be a place where the troubles and cares of life are ended. This will be the land described in this song:

  "Beyond this land of parting, losing, and leaving,
  Far beyond the losses, darkening this,
  And far beyond the taking and the bereaving
  Lies the summerland of bliss."

- A place of rest (Rev. 14:13). When one has worked long hours day after day, his spirit yearns for a place of rest. Heaven is described as a place of everlasting rest, where all of one's labors and trials are over.
- A place of perfect safety. Heaven is a city where the gates are never closed (Rev. 21:25). The gates of a city were closed in time of siege. The point is that the Devil has been destroyed and God's people will never again be subjected to the Devil's temptations. In the song "Where The Roses Never Fade," The poet wrote,

  "In this world we have our troubles,
  Satan's snares we must evade;
  We'll be free from all temptations
  Where the roses never fade."

- Tabernacling with God (Rev. 21:3). In the Old Testament, the Lord described his on-going fellowship with the children of Israel by having his presence in the Tabernacle. Heaven is described as a place where God tabernacles among men.
- Paradise (Rev. 2:7). The figure of heaven as "paradise" calls us back to the beautiful Garden of Eden which God prepared for man's life on earth. It was lost because of sin but is regained through Christ.
- Access to the water of life (Rev. 21:6; 22:1, 17) and the tree of life (Rev. 2:7; 22:2, 14). The "tree of life" reminds us of that which was available to man in the Garden of Eden that enabled him to live forever (Gen. 2:9; 3:22, 24).
- Eternal life (Mark 10:30; John 3:15-16; Rom. 2:7). Life is being in fellowship with God (contrast to being "dead" in sin). Eternal life is a spiritual fellowship that never ends.

NOTES

The Beauty of Heaven

The New Jerusalem is described in glorious terms in Revelation 21. It is a place prepared for the saints, like a bride adorned for her husband (21:2). The wall is of jasper and its streets are of pure gold. Its foundations are made of every kind of precious stone: jasper, sapphire, chalcedony, emerald, sardonyx, sardius, chrysolyte, beryl, topaz, chrysoprasus, jacinth, amethyst. Its gates are made of pearls and its streets of gold (see Rev. 21:11-21). Although this is probably not to be understood literally, the message of these figures of speech is that heaven is more beautiful than our minds can imagine. It exceeds the beauty of the sun glistening on the icicles following an ice storm, the rainbow of colors of the leaves in the Smoky Mountains in October, the beautiful Niagara Falls, or anything else to compare on earth. Indeed, this is the beautiful "paradise valley."

Conclusion

John Brown wrote,

> The life of the saints . . . is always in some degree, often in a high degree, a scene of toil and suffering, and the closing part of it is sometimes remarkably characterized by restlessness and agony. His passage over the sea of life is frequently stormy throughout, and sometimes becomes peculiarly tempestuous toward its termination. But at death, "God maketh the storm a calm, and the waves thereof are still." Then is the Christian mariner glad because he is quiet. His weather-beaten vessel is moored in a safe haven, never more to return to the tossing of the wasteful ocean. "There the wicked cease from troubling, and there the weary are at rest." The Christian 'enters into peace—he rests in his bed—each one that walketh in his uprightness." His "end" is, emphatically, "peace" (quoted in Wilbur Smith, *The Biblical Doctrine of Heaven,* 157).

Ronnie Milliner asked if we truly long for heaven as he wrote the following:

> Are we truthful when we sing, "What a joy 'twill be when I wake to see Him for whom my heart is burning! Nevermore to sigh, nevermore to die — For that day my heart is yearning"? Or what about, "Closing my eyes at eve and thinking of heaven's grace, Longing to see my Lord, yes, meeting Him face to face." Let us ever raise our voices to proclaim, "O Zion, Zion, I long thy gates to see; O Zion, Zion, When shall I dwell in thee?" Truly, "sing to me of Heaven" ought to be on the lips of every Christian ("Sing To Me of Heaven," *Guardian of Truth* [August 20, 1987], XXXI: 16, p. 16).

NOTES

Questions

1. List three uses of the word "heaven."

   a. ______________________________

   b. ______________________________

   c. ______________________________

2. Who will be in heaven? ______________________________

   ____

3. What is the significance of "dwelling with God" (Rev. 21:2)? ______________________________

   ____

4. Who are excluded from heaven (Rev. 21:8, 27)? ______________________________

   ____

5. Why is the absence of sin in heaven part of what makes it attractive (Rev. 21:8, 27)? ____________

   ____

   ____

6. In what ways is heaven like:

   a. A wedding feast (Matt. 22:1-14; 25:10)? ______________________________

      ____

   b. Inheriting a kingdom (Matt. 25:34)? ______________________________

      ____

   c. A great banquet (Matt. 25:11)? ______________________________

      ____

   d. A reward (Matt. 5:12; 10:42)? ______________________________

      ____

   e. Ruling over a city (Luke 12:43-44; 19:17, 19)? ______________________________

      ____

   f. Home (Eccl. 12:7)? ______________________________

      ____

g. A reunion (1 Thess. 4:13-18)? ______

______

h. Jerusalem (Rev. 3:21; 21:2, 10)? ______

______

i. A place where there is no night (Rev. 21:25; 22:5)? ______

______

j. Rest (Rev. 14:13)? ______

______

7. What do the following images of heaven teach:

a. Gates of the city are never closed (Rev. 21:25)? ______

______

b. Access to the water of life and tree of life (Rev. 21:6-7; 22:1-2, 14, 17)? ______

______

c. Paradise (Rev. 2:7)? ______

______

8. Why do you want to go to heaven? ______

______

Lesson 12

Realized Eschatology: The A.D. 70 Doctrine

This lesson begins an examination of several false doctrines relative to the end times. Throughout time, brethren have been troubled by some among us who have preached false doctrines relative to what will happen at the end of time. Among those false doctrines that have troubled brethren are the A.D. 70 Doctrine and premillennial theories. This lesson will discuss the A.D. 70 doctrine and subsequent lessons will cover various aspects of premillennialism.

The A.D. 70 doctrine can be summarized from the masthead of the magazine that propagates their theory, *Studies in Bible Prophecy* (IX:2 [March-May 1987]:

> The Holy Scriptures teach that the second coming of Christ, including the establishment of the eternal kingdom, the day of judgment, the end of the world and the resurrection of the dead, occurred with the fall of Judaism in 70 A.D.

This view is called the preterist view. A "preterist" is "one whose chief interest and pleasures are in the past." When applied to theology, the preterist view refers to "one who believes that the prophecies of the Apocalypse (Revelation) have already been fulfilled." Briefly stated, the A.D. 70 doctrine teaches that the Lord's second coming occurred in A.D. 70 when he brought judgment against the nation of Israel and destroyed the city of Jerusalem. That was the end of the world. The resurrection of the dead occurred at that time. What lies ahead for Christians? Most preterists believe that, at death, the bodiless spirit goes to be with God forever. There is no future second coming or resurrection. We need to examine this doctrine because it undermines the "one hope" of the Christian faith (Eph. 4:4).

. . . the A.D. 70 doctrine teaches that the Lord's second coming occurred in A.D. 70 when he brought judgment against the nation of Israel and destroyed the city of Jerusalem. That was the end of the world. The resurrection of the dead occurred at that time.

The Bible Speaks of the Fall of Jerusalem as a Judgment of God

Most of the passages that are used to teach the A.D. 70 doctrine rely upon texts related to the destruction of the city of Jerusalem (Matt. 24; Mark 13; Luke 21). We need to recognize that the destruction of the city of Jerusalem was indeed a judgment from God, although it was not the final judgment.

The fall of Jerusalem was prophesied in the gospels (Matt. 24 [and its parallels in Mark 13 and Luke 21]; 21:33-44; 22:1-14, esp. v. 7). The Lord's coming in judgment against Jerusalem is sometimes described in typical apocalyptic language (Matt. 24:29-30).[1] The judgment against the city of Jerusalem in A.D. 70 was the Lord's judgment (Matt. 24:30). We need to understand that the word "judgment" can be used of temporal judgments as well as the final judgment (cf. Rev. 14:7-8). Just like other judgments against nations were the Lord's judgment, the destruction of Jerusalem is described as the Lord's judgment (Matt. 10:23; 24:29f).

The A.D. 70 doctrine advocates make the Lord's judgment of Jerusalem in A.D. 70 the central hub of the Bible. Here are some of the

[1] Most people are unfamiliar with apocalyptic language. For examples of apocalyptic language being used to describe a temporal judgment against a nation, see Isaiah 13:9-13; Ezekiel 32:7; Joel 2:10; 3:4. Sometimes one who reads such language immediately thinks the subject is the Lord's second coming without carefully considering the context of the passage.

things they believe happened at the destruction of Jerusalem in A.D. 70.

1. This is the time when the Jewish dispensation ended and the Christian dispensation began. The end of the Jewish age is the "end of the world" of Bible prophecy. In contrast to this, Hebrews 9:15-17 says the old covenant ended at Jesus' death.

2. This is the end of all inspiration, miraculous gifts, and prophecy. Every prophecy in the Bible is fulfilled in this judgment. This view demands that every New Testament book have been written before A.D. 70, a view not shared by most N.T. scholars.[2]

3. The coming of the Lord in destruction of the city was the Lord's second coming.

4. The Christian dispensation is the delivered up kingdom of God. The "resurrection from the dead" is the establishment of the spiritual body that was raised up after the physical body (Israel or Jerusalem) was destroyed. (Note how "resurrection of the dead" has been redefined.)

Indeed, the central events of Bible history shift from the cross and from Pentecost to the destruction of Jerusalem in A.D. 70.

The A.D. 70 advocates make a major blunder in understanding all of the references to Christ's comings to mean the judgment against Jerusalem in A.D. 70. Here are some other comings of Christ:

- He came to earth as a human being (Gen. 49:10; Luke 19:10).
- He came in his kingdom on Pentecost (Matt. 16:28; John 14:18).
- He came in judgment against Jerusalem (Matt. 10:23; 24:30).
- He comes in salvation (John 14:23).
- He comes in discipline against a local church (Rev. 2:5).
- He comes in fellowship (Rev. 3:20).
- He will come in a universal judgment at the last day (Matt. 16:27).

One must study the context of the various passages that refer to Jesus' coming to ascertain to which coming one is referring.

These Things Are Yet to Come

The Scriptures do not indicate that the end of all things has already occurred. Rather, the Scriptures tell us that there are several things yet to come. Here are some things that are yet to come:

1. The Lord's second coming. Although we recognize that Jesus' coming in judgment was a "coming" of the Lord, it was not the "second coming" (Heb. 9:27-28). Here are some things spoken about the second coming: (a) Jesus promised to come again and take his saints to be with him forever (John 14:1-3); (b) The angels promised that he would come again with the clouds of heaven, just as he ascended (Acts 1:11); (c) We are to become like Christ when he comes (1 John 3:2); (d) 1 Thessalonians 4:13-18 promises a series of events to occur at that time (the Lord will descend from heaven with a shout, the trumpet of God shall sound, the dead will arise, and the living saints will be caught up with Christ in the air); (e)

[2] Though essential for the A.D. 70 doctrine, the view that all of the New Testament was completed by A.D. 70 is not essential for the view that we are defending in this class. The books of the New Testament not thought to have been written by A.D. 70 are John, 1-3 John, Jude, and Revelation. The passages in these books that speak of a future coming of the Lord devastate the A.D. 70. Therefore, preterists are forced to take the position that these books were written before A.D. 70.

NOTES

2 Thessalonians 1:7-9 also relates things to occur at the coming (the righteous will be given rest, the Lord will come in flaming fire taking vengeance on those who do not know God and have not obeyed the gospel, they will be punished with everlasting destruction from the presence of the Lord, and the saints will be glorified); (f) Every eye will see Jesus when he comes again (Rev. 1:7).

If these things happened in A.D. 70, these consequences follow: (a) Every eye has seen Jesus. Have you? Inasmuch as he has already come, according to preterist eschatology, there is no authority to sing "We Shall See the King Someday." We missed the Lord's second coming! (b) There is no authority to partake of the Lord's supper since we are to partake of it "till he comes" (1 Cor. 11:26). (c) There is no reason to baptize people because Christ has only promised to be with us until the "end of the world," which A.D. 70 advocates say occurred in A.D. 70 (Matt. 28:18-20). The Lord expects men to teach the gospel until his second coming. At that time, the day of grace ends and the door of salvation is shut. If the second coming occurred in A.D. 70, the door of salvation was shut at that time. If Jesus' coming in judgment at A.D. 70 fulfilled his promise to come again, there is no future coming to look toward.

2. The kingdom of Christ has already reached its eternal reality. The church is the spiritual kingdom (Matt. 16:18). We become citizens of it by obeying the gospel (John 3:1-5). This kingdom is an eternal kingdom, one that "cannot be moved" (Heb. 12:28). It will be delivered up to the Father at the Lord's second coming, at which time Jesus' reign is over (1 Cor. 15:24-28). Entrance into the heavenly kingdom is a synonym for heaven (2 Pet. 1:11). If the kingdom is already come in its heavenly fulness, what we are presently experiencing in the spiritual blessings of our church relationship is all the heaven there is.

3. The resurrection of the body from the dead. The Bible speaks words of comfort to prepare us for death and to comfort our loved ones after death. It promises a resurrection of the body (1 Thess. 4:13-17; 1 Cor. 15:42-44). According to the A.D. 70 theory, the resurrection of the dead occurred when the church emerged out of the spiritually dead and destroyed kingdom of Israel. In this case, the resurrection has already occurred. If there is anything left to hope for, it is an eternal existence as bodiless souls, a distinctly different hope from that offered by Christ. The resurrection of Jesus' body from the dead was the firstfruits of our own resurrection (1 Cor. 15:20-23). We shall have a body like that of Jesus (Phil. 3:20-21).

The proponents of the A.D. 70 doctrine are like Hymenaeus and Philetus who taught that the resurrection was already past (2 Tim. 2:18). They leave us with a gospel that has hope only in this life, making us of all men most pitiable (1 Cor. 15:19).

Physical evidences demonstrate that the resurrection did not occur in A.D. 70. If the dead were raised in A.D. there should be no physical bodies found in tombs that date before A.D. 70. The existence of Egyptian mummies and other ancient bodies demonstrates that the resurrection did not occur in A.D. 70.

4. The destruction of the heavens and earth. The heavens and earth are to be destroyed at the Lord's second coming (2 Pet. 3:9-12). But the A.D. 70 doctrine teaches that the heavens and earth have already been destroyed. They re-define "heavens and earth" to mean the Jewish state. If one will allow a person to give special definitions to any words that he chooses, that person can prove anything! If the end of the world has already come, Jesus is no longer with us (Matt. 28:20).

NOTES

5. The judgment. The judgment will occur when Jesus comes back again (Matt. 25:31f; John 5:28-29). But the A.D. 70 doctrine makes the judgment refer to the Lord's judgment on the nation of Israel when he destroyed Jerusalem. Although that was a judgment, it was not the final judgment at the end of the world. There is no need to sing "Prepare to Meet Thy God" or "There's A Great Day Coming" if there is no future judgment.

Here is the mummy of an Egyptian man that is displayed at the British Museum. He lived centuries before Christ. The realized eschatology advocates say that the resurrection occurred in A.D. 70. The Bible teaches that the good and bad will be raised at the same time (John 5:28-29). Why then, are there mummies if the resurrection has already occurred? Whether this man was good or bad, he should have been raised in A.D. 70, if the teaching of the realized eschatology advocates are right. The fact that he was not raised shows that the resurrection has not yet come and that their theory is mistaken.

Conclusion

The doctrine that teaches "the second coming, the establishment of the eternal kingdom, the day of judgment, the end of the world and the resurrection of the dead, occurred with the fall of Judaism in A.D. 70" is false. It is not a harmless doctrine because it directly contradicts the plain statements of Scripture and undermines the Christian's one hope.

NOTES

Questions

1. What are the major beliefs of realized eschatology? ______________________________

____

____

2. Why is it called a "preterist" view? ______________________________

____

3. Why did God bring judgment against Jerusalem in A.D. 70 (Matt. 21:33-44)? ______________

____

4. What happened to God's relationship with Israel after the death of Christ (Matt. 21:43)? ________

____

5. According to Matthew 22:1-7, why did God destroy Jerusalem? ______________________

____

6. Why do preterists have to believe that the New Testament was completed by A.D. 70? ________

____

7. List four comings of the Lord other than the second coming.

   a. ____

   b. ____

   c. ____

   d. ____

8. What does the A.D. 70 doctrine teach about the second coming? ______________________

____

9. What verses show that the second coming did not occur in A.D. 70? ______________________

____

10. In what sense is the kingdom of heaven a present reality (Matt. 16:18)? ________________

____

11. In what sense is the kingdom of heaven a future blessing (1 Cor. 15:24-28; 2 Pet. 1:11)? ________

____

12. What physical evidence shows that the resurrection of the dead did not occur in A.D. 70? _______

____

13. If there is no future resurrection of the dead, what is man's state in eternity? ____________________

____

14. What doctrine did Hymenaeus and Philetus teach (2 Tim. 2:18)? ____________________

____

15. What is the meaning of "resurrection of the dead" according to A.D. 70 advocates? ____________

____

16. What do preterists believe about the destruction of the heavens and earth? ____________________

____

17. What do preterists believe about the judgment? ____________________

____

Lesson 13

Matthew 24-25

Both those who teach the A.D. 70 doctrine of realized eschatology and premillennialists abuse Matthew 24 and 25. The realized eschatologists teach that the prophecies of both chapters were fulfilled at the destruction of Jerusalem in A.D. 70 and premillennialists use the prophecies of the destruction of Jerusalem as signs of the imminent second coming of Christ and the coming *Great Tribulation*. The so-called Jehovah's Witnesses who do much door-to-door teaching, usually begin their presentation with the "signs of the times" material based on Matthew 24 to assert that the time of the end of the world is near. Some modernists misinterpret the chapters to teach that Jesus was mistaken in believing the end of the world was imminent in his own age.

One cannot adequately cover the subject of eschatology without a study of these two chapters. This lesson will examine these two chapters to learn what Jesus was saying to the audience who heard him speak.[1]

The Contextual Setting of Matthew 24

On Sunday of the last week before his death, Jesus triumphantly entered Jerusalem (Matt. 21:1-11). He was riding on a colt, the foal of an ass, and the people were shouting, "Hosanna to the son of David: Blessed is he that cometh in the name of the Lord; Hosanna in the highest" (Matt. 21:9). Within a week, a mob shouted, "Crucify him." Jesus had several direct conflicts with the Jewish leaders that week (Matt. 22-23).

The events which scholars suppose to have occurred on Tuesday of the same week are: (1) The authority of Jesus was challenged following the cleansing of the temple on Monday (Matt. 21:12-17, 23-27). (2) The Jewish leaders questioned Jesus as they sought to ensnare him in his speech while he was teaching in the temple (Matt. 22:15-40). (3) Jesus answered their questions and then asked them a question they could not answer about the Christ being both the Son of David and David's Lord (Matt. 22:41-46). (4) Jesus denounced the Pharisees (Matt. 23:1-39). (5) The incident of Jesus witnessing the widow giving two mites (Luke 21:1-3). Following these events, Jesus probably walked out of the temple where the conversation of Matthew 24:1-2 occurred. When Jesus and his disciples arrived on the Mount of Olives, Jesus gave this discourse which continues through Matthew 25:46.

There are two judgments under discussion in these chapters. The first is a prediction of the destruction of Jerusalem in A.D. 70. The second is a prediction of the judgment at the second coming of Christ, at the end of the world.

Questions Discussed in Matthew 24:3

There were three questions under discussion in this section: (1) When shall the stones of the temple be overturned? (2) What shall be the signs of thy coming in judgment against Jerusalem? (3) What shall be the signs of the end of the world? Most Jews probably felt that the world would end when and if Jerusalem were destroyed. However, Jesus clearly distinguishes between the things that will occur at the destruction of Jerusalem and the end of the world.

There are two judgments under discussion in these chapters. The first is a prediction of the

[1] Parallel accounts of this material are recorded in Mark 13 and Luke 21. We will confine this study to Matthew's account, but one should note the parallel texts.

Judgment on Jerusalem	Judgment at the End of the World
Preceded by signs (24:5-15)	No signs of the Lord's coming judgment; like the days of Noah (24:36-39)
Can be escaped by flight (24:16)	Cannot be escaped (24:42; 25:31)
No personal coming of Christ (24:23)	Personal coming of Christ (24:44)
Judgment on earth (24:15)	Judgment in heaven (25:31)

destruction of Jerusalem in A.D. 70. The second is a prediction of the judgment at the second coming of Christ, at the end of the world.

Matthew 24 is divided into two sections. One should take notice of the difference in the language of the two sections. Verses 15-21 especially discuss a local judgment from which man can flee. Verses 37-44 describe a universal judgment from which none can flee. In the chart above on this page, notice the differences between the two judgments.

The two sections of Jesus' lesson are separated by a time text. "Verily I say unto you, This generation shall not pass, till all these things be fulfilled" (Matt. 24:34). The things discussed before v. 34 would occur within that "generation." The word "generation" (*genea*) means "the whole multitude of men living at the same time, ... an age (i.e. the time ordinarily occupied by each successive generation), the space of from 30 to 33 years" (Thayer, 112). Jesus was saying that the events described prior to v. 34 would transpire within the lifetime of those alive at that moment. The word *genea* is never used to mean the human race or the nation of Israel. Jesus was so certain that what he predicted would occur that he said, "Heaven and earth shall pass away, but my words shall not pass away" (Matt. 24:35).

The only part of the Temple that survived the destruction of Jerusalem in A.D. 70 was the western retaining wall for the Temple Mount. The place is known as the Wailing Wall and is a popular place for worship for modern Jews. The large stones are evidence of Herodian construction.

The subject matter changes in Matthew 24:36 to speak of a judgment that will occur without warning. "But of that day and hour knoweth no man, no, not the angels of heaven, but my Father only" (Matt. 24:36). The judgment that will occur without warning is further described in 24:37-25:46. It is the judgment at the end of the world. One can never unravel and understand Matthew 24-25 without distinguishing these two judgments.

NOTES

The Destruction of Jerusalem (24:4-34)

Archaeologists have uncovered one of the houses destroyed in the destruction of Jerusalem. It is known as the Burnt House. The house belonged to a person named Bar Kathros, a member of the high priestly family.

Jesus gave a number of signs to let the disciples know when the city of Jerusalem would be destroyed. Here is a list of those signs:

1. Misleading signs of the end (24:4-13). How often these verses are read as signs of the end of the world! These signs were not indicative of the destruction of Jerusalem but were to occur prior to the destruction. Jesus warned his disciples not to be carried away by these following signs.

(a) False Christs were to come (24:5). The word "christ" is used to refer to the "anointed one" who was foretold in the Old Testament. Many charismatic leaders would come, each one asserting that he was the christ. Jesus foretold this so that the disciples would not be deceived by those who came making this claim. Josephus mentions several men who came in that era making that claim.

(b) "Wars and rumors of wars" (24:6-7). The Roman period of peace, later known as the *Pax Romana,* was coming to an end. Tension began to develop around A.D. 50 which culminated in the Jewish wars of A.D. 65-73. William R. Kimball cited evidences of this in relating the following: an uprising in Caesarea that cost the lives of 20,000 Jews, an incident in Scythopolis that resulted in 13,000 being slain, an outbreak in Alexandria, Egypt that killed 50,000 Jews, and an incident in Damascus, Syria that cost 10,000 Jews their lives (*What The Bible Says About the Great Tribulation,* 24).

(c) Famines (24:7). The prophet Agabus specifically mentioned a famine in the days of Claudius Caesar (see Acts 11:27-30).

(d) Earthquakes (24:7). Archaeological research has uncovered a disastrous earthquake which occurred in approximately A.D. 37 at Wadi Qumran. Josephus tells of a major earthquake in Judea which was accompanied by violent winds, vehement showers, continual lightnings, and terrible thunderings (*Wars*, Book 4, Ch. 4.5). Others could have occurred which left no visible signs or written records after 2000 years.

(e) Persecutions of the saints (24:9-10). Early persecutions of the church mentioned in

NOTES

the New Testament include these: (1) Apostles were beaten and threatened (Acts 5:40-41); (2) Stephen was murdered and a general persecution occurred (Acts 7:59-8:4); (3) Herod Agrippa I led a persecution in Acts 12 that resulted in the death of James; (4) Nero's persecution (54-68 A.D.).

(f) False prophets would arise (24:11). The letters to the churches mention various false prophets.

(g) Many would apostatize (24:12).

(h) Only those who endured to the end would be saved (24:13).

All of these signs would occur before the end of Jerusalem was to occur. The disciples were not to think that the end of Jerusalem was imminent as they witnessed these things happening.

2. Real signs of the end of Jerusalem (24:14-16). Jesus gave these signs to show when the destruction would occur.

(a) The gospel first had to be preached to all nations (see Col. 1:23). This is not to be understood in the sense that every man under heaven would hear the gospel, but that the gospel would be taken to the Gentiles.

(b) The abomination of desolation foretold by Daniel would stand in the holy place. Here is a reference to the approach of the Roman army (Luke 21:20). Josephus records an incident in which Pilate erected the ensigns of the Roman government in the Temple (*Antiquities of the Jews* Book 18, Chapter 3, 1). The Roman general Cestius attacked the city in approximately A.D. 66 before the fall of Jerusalem and withdrew from the city for no apparent reason. Samuel Burder added this note to Josephus' record of this incident:

> There may another very important, and very providential reason be here assigned, for this stand and foolish retreat of Cestius's: which, if Josephus had been a Christian, he might probably have taken notice of also: and that is, the affording the Jewish Christians in the city an opportunity of calling to mind the prediction and caution given them by Christ about 33½ years before; that when they should see the abomination of desolation, [the idolatrous Roman armies, with the images of their idols, in their ensigns, ready to lay Jerusalem desolate,] stand where it ought not; or, in the holy place. Or, when they should see Jerusalem compassed with armies, they should then flee to the mountains. By complying with which those Jewish Christians fled to the mountains of Perea, and escaped the destruction (*Josephus: Wars of the Jews*, note on Book II, Chap. XIX, p. 273).

3. Great tribulation (24:17-22). Christians were instructed to flee from Jerusalem and Judea into the the mountains in order to avoid the fate by the Roman army.[2] So terrible would be the tribulation, that those who had children or were pregnant would be hindered in their flight. They should pray that their flight should not occur in the winter nor on the Sabbath day because of natural difficulties which would develop. The city underwent the world's worse tribulation. Josephus' account tells of cannibalism and terror within the city. Fortunately, the time was shortened for the elect's sake.

4. There would be no personal coming of Jesus during the seige (24:23-28). Notice the adverb "then" in 24:23 indicates that although false Christs arise, Jesus would not return at that time. Many would be led away by those false prophets. When Jesus comes, his presence cannot be misinterpreted. Notice his comparison of his coming to lightning which is clearly visible to all

[2] Eusebius wrote, "The whole body, however, of the church at Jerusalem, having been commanded by a divine revelation, given to men of approved piety there before the war, removed from the city, and dwelt at a certain town beyond Jordan, called Pella" (*Ecclesiastical History* Book III, Chap. 5, p. 86).

NOTES

men and no one needs anyone to tell him that it has occurred. Similarly, where the carcass is, the vultures shall be gathered.

5. Signs in the sun, moon, and stars (24:29-3l). The word "immediately" prevents these verses having application to the second coming of Jesus and must, therefore, in some way relate to the destruction of Jerusalem. These are the verses hardest for men to understand about the destruction of Jerusalem because of the use of apocalyptic language. In the Old Testament, such language is used to refer to (a) the fall of Babylon (Isa. 13:10), (b) the fall of Egypt (Ezek. 32:7, 8), (c) the locust plague, Pentecost, and the battle in the valley of Jehoshaphat (Joel 2:10, 30-31, 3:15). This language discusses the magnitude of the fall of each of these powerful nations and must mean the same thing here. The sun, moon, and stars may be a reference to fall of the Jewish leaders, symbolizing the destruction of the nation. The collapse of the nation is like the sun, moon, and stars falling.

The destruction of Jerusalem was a "sign of the Son of Man in heaven." What happened at the destruction of Jerusalem is proof that Jesus sits at the right hand of God. Jesus was coming on the clouds of heaven in judgment against Jerusalem (24:30).[3] J. Marcellus Kik observed, "One of the first manifestations of the power and the glory of the Messiah was the destruction of the city that refused to accept him as King and Savior. This act of judgment gave evidence that all power had indeed been given unto him" (*Matthew XXIV,* 85).

(6) The gathering of the elect. These verses indicate the spread of the gospel into all the world as a consequence of the fall of Jerusalem (cf. Rom. 11:11).

The parable of the fig tree (vv. 32-33) indicates that, through these signs, one could foresee the destruction of Jerusalem enough to make arrangements to leave the city before they were harmed. All of the above signs were to occur within one generation (Matt. 24:34).

Universal Judgment (24:35-25:46)

Although Jesus gave signs of the destruction of Jerusalem, for the end of the world, he gave no such signs (Matt. 24:35-36). No man knows when the second coming will occur (24:36). He only said that it will come without warning, just as the destruction of the flood came without warning (24:37-44). A great separation of men will occur when Jesus' second coming happens (24:41-44). This separation is further described in Matthew 25. Matthew 25 gives the following parables depicting the end of the world: (a) The faithful and unfaithful servants (24:45-5l); (b) The ten virgins (25:1-13); (c) The talents (25:14-30); (d) Separation of sheep and goats at judgment (25:31-46).[4]

Conclusion

A proper understanding of these verses is essential in order to avoid the errors of the premillennialist doctrine of the Jehovah's Witnesses and other groups as well as the false teaching of the realized eschatologists.

---

[3] Other verses show God coming on clouds in judgment against nations (Isa. 19:1; cf. Matt. 26:64).

[4] To be consistent in their interpretation of Matthew 24, realized eschatologists (those holding the A.D. 70 doctrine) have to make these parables speak of the judgment against Jerusalem, resulting in the claim that the end of the world, the second coming, and resurrection all occurred in A.D. 70.

NOTES

Questions

1. How do the following groups abuse Matthew 24-25?
   a. Realized eschatologists? ______
   b. Premillennialists? ______
   c. Modernists? ______
2. Where are the parallel accounts to Matthew 24 found? ______
3. List the questions Jesus answered in Matthew 24 (24:3):
   a. ______
   b. ______
   c. ______
4. What two judgments are described in Matthew 24-25? ______

   ______

   ______
5. What verse separates those two judgments? ______
6. Within what time frame was 24:1-34 to be fulfilled (24:34)? ______
7. List several things that Jesus said would occur before the "end" which were not signs of his return:
   a. ______
   b. ______
   c. ______
   d. ______
   e. ______
   f. ______
   g. ______
   h. ______
8. What were the true signs of the "end" (24:14-16)? ______

   ______
9. How could Christians escape the tribulations of the "end" (24:17-22)? ______

10. Did Jesus come back to earth in A.D. 70 (24:23)? ____________________

11. How is Jesus' second coming like lightning (24:27)? ____________________

12. What message is conveyed in the apocalyptic language of 24:29-31? ____________________

13. How did the destruction of Jerusalem show Christ is reigning in heaven (24:30-31)? ____________________

14. Explain the parable of the fig tree (24:32-33). ____________________

15. What are the signs of Jesus' second coming (24:36ff.)? ____________________

16. Who knows when Jesus' second coming will occur (24:36)? ____________________

17. What should Christians do to escape the judgment of the second coming (24:42)? ____________________

Lesson 14

Millennial Theories

In this study of eschatology, we have emphasized that the Bible teaches that the following sequence of events will transpire at the end of the age:

- The second coming of Jesus.
- The resurrection of the dead
- The destruction of the heavens and earth
- Judgment
- Heaven and hell

Many who believe in the inspiration of the Bible hold a different belief about the end times. It is generally described by such terms as "premillennialism" or "dispensationalism." Because every teacher of premillennialism has some different twist to everyone else, one would expect that some of the details may vary from one premillennialist to another.

Definition of Terms

To understand millennialism, one must know some terms that are frequently used in these discussions. Given below are some terms that reflect the different beliefs that various people hold.

1. Postmillennialism: "the belief that the second coming of Christ will follow the millennium" (Webster). "An optimistic type of theology which predicts a 'golden age,' a Christianized millennium of predominantly human achievement before the Second Advent and the subsequent, eternal reign" (*The New International Dictionary of the Christian Church*, J.D. Douglas, editor, 794). Some of our religious ancestors, such as Alexander Campbell who published a paper entitled *Millennial Harbinger*, held this view of the end times. Although he was mistaken in his belief, his doctrines did not undermine the biblical doctrine of the church.

2. Premillennialism: "the doctrine that the reappearance of Christ on earth will precede the millennium" (Webster). "The view which asserts that Christ will come a second time before the 1,000 years of his millennial rule, upholds a general chiliastic theology of Millennialism, and places the rapture of the saints, the first resurrection, the tribulation, and the Second Advent before the Millennium in prophetic time sequence, with the brief release of bound Satan, the second resurrection, and Last Judgment afterward" (*The New International Dictionary of the Christian Church*, J.D. Douglas, editor, 798-799).

3. Amillennialism "denies such a thousand year reign: . . .stresses that the Apocalypse normally treats numbers symbolically. The binding of Satan for a thousand years simply

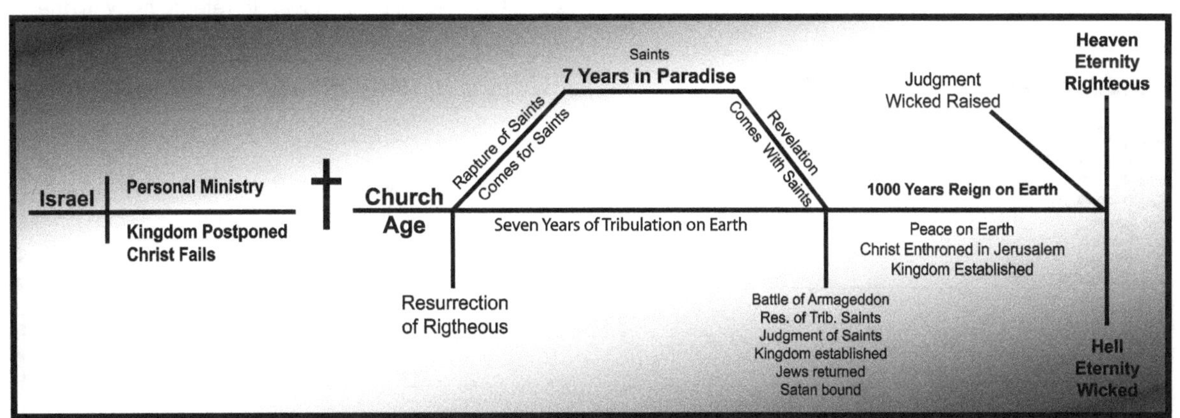

means that he is completely bound; this has been effected through the victory of Calvary" (*The New International Dictionary of the Christian Church*, J.D. Douglas, editor, 36). We are amillennialists in our convictions about the end times.

The Theory of Premillennialism

The theory of premillennialism may be summarized as follows:

- When Jesus came to the earth, he came with the intention of establishing an earthly kingdom.
- The Jews rejected Jesus and had him crucified.
- God instituted an alternative plan, to establish a spiritual kingdom, the church.
- The church age will last until the earthly kingdom is established.
- At sometime in the near future, Jesus will come back and silently raise the righteous dead and rapture the living saints from the earth.
- Seven years of tribulation will be experienced on earth when Satan is loosed for a little season.
- Jesus will return to earth, bringing his saints with him. The battle of Armageddon will be fought. Satan will be defeated. Jesus will establish an earthly kingdom over which he will reign for 1000 years.
- At the end of the 1000 year reign, the wicked dead will be raised and judgment will be given to all men.
- The righteous will go to heaven and the wicked will go to hell.

What Is Wrong with Premillennialism

1. It teaches that Christ came to establish an earthly kingdom. The kingdom Christ came to establish was spiritual (Luke 17:20-21; John 18:36-37; 3:3-5; Rom. 14:17). The kingdom is the church (Matt. 16:16-18). It was established on Pentecost (Mark 9:1; Acts 1:8; 2:1-4, 47). In this respect, the kingdom has come (Acts 8:12; 28:23; Col. 1:13-14; Heb. 12:28; Rev. 1:9).[1] The doctrine that Jesus came to establish an earthly kingdom is wrong. Jesus did not come in his first coming and will not come in his second coming for the purpose of establishing an earthly kingdom.

Jesus did not come in his first coming and will not come in his second coming for the purpose of establishing an earthly kingdom.

2. It teaches that Jesus failed in what he set out to do—to establish an earthly kingdom. The Bible teaches that Christ would not fail in his mission (Ps. 2). If Jesus failed when he came to establish the kingdom on his first coming, what guarantee would we have that he would be able to accomplish at his second coming what he failed to do the first time? The very idea that the Son of God failed in what he purposed to do is blasphemous.

[1] The "kingdom" is used in two senses: (a) To refer to the spiritual kingdom, known as the church (Matt. 16:18) and (b) To refer to the eternal kingdom of heaven (2 Pet. 1:11). In respect to the use of "kingdom" as church, that kingdom came on Pentecost (Mark 9:1; Acts 2). In respect to the use of "kingdom" to refer to heaven, the kingdom is still anticipated.

NOTES

3. It teaches, by logical implication, that Christ is not presently reigning as king, by denying that the kingdom is presently established. If there is no kingdom, how could there be a king over that kingdom? Hence, the theory implies that Jesus is not presently King of kings and Lord of lords (1 Tim. 6:15). If there is no kingdom, how could one be a citizen of it (John 3:3-5)? Jesus is presently reigning (Heb. 10:10-13; 1:3, 13; 1 Cor. 15:26-26; 1 Tim. 6:15; Acts 2:29-36; Rev. 3:21). (Note the implications of the fact that Jesus is presently reigning for the 1000 year reign of Christ in Revelation 20.) The Scriptures show that: (a) Jesus is reigning on the throne of David (Isa. 9:6-7; Luke 1:32-33; Acts 2:29-31); (b) He has the key of David (Isa. 22:22; Rev. 3:7); (c) He rules in the midst of his enemies (Ps. 110). His is not a reign in total utopia. (d) Jesus has all authority (Matt. 28:18; Eph. 1:19-22; Col. 2:16).

4. It teaches that Jesus' death on the cross was not Christ's intended purpose for coming to the earth. Jesus expressed that he came to save the lost (Luke 19:10) and prophesied of his own death (Matt. 16:21). God's plan to save mankind through the death of his Son was purposed before the creation of the world (Rev. 13:8).

5. It teaches that the church, rather than being a part of God's eternal purpose, is an accident (contrast Eph. 3:8-11). The church age was necessary because the Jews rejected Jesus as the Christ.

6. It teaches an imminent coming of the Lord based on a misinterpretation of Matthew 24. For as long as I can remember, premillennialists have been preaching that the second coming is near. Prophetic speculation is part of the history of the church. William G. Miller predicted the Lord's coming on March 23, 1843, and on March 23, 1844, and a third time on October 22, 1844. Ellen G. White reinterpreted Miller's predictions to make them refer to activities in heaven. Thus was founded the Seventh Day Adventists. Charles Taze Russell (Jehovah's Witnesses) predicted the Lord's coming in 1914. Edgar C. Whisenant mailed out a book to every church in the U.S. announcing *88 Reasons Why the Rapture Could Be in 1988.* Billy Graham preached that the second coming was imminent when I was a boy growing up. Misinterpretation of Matthew 24 to find evidence of the imminent return of Christ is a feature of premillennialism. The truth is that no one knows when Christ will come again (Matt. 24:36).

Which Churches Believe in Premillennialism?

- **Southern Baptists**
- **Pentecostals**
- **Some Independent Christian Churches**
- **Premillennial Churches of Christ**

7. Premillennialism has many problems of correct Bible exegesis. (a) It demands several resurrections, including the rapture, after the tribulation period, and after the millennium (the general resurrection). In contrast, the Scriptures teach that there is but one resurrection (John 5:28-29; 2 Thess. 1:6-9; Acts 24:15).

(b) It teaches more than one "second coming." Here are the comings premillennialists believe in: (1) a secret coming at the rapture. At this time, the saints will be taken to heaven where they will stay for seven years and then return to this earth. (Have you seen the bumper sticker that reads: "In case of rapture, this car will be

NOTES

unmanned"?) (2) A coming to establish his earthly kingdom. How many "second comings" are there?

(c) It gives the "last day" a new meaning. Resurrection (John 11:24; 6:39-40) and judgment (John 12:48) are to occur on the last day. Premillennialism believes that there is a thousand year reign of Christ between resurrection and judgment. That would demand 365,000 "last days"!

(d) It offers salvation to people after the second coming. The day of grace is over when Christ comes again (Matt. 25:6-10; Luke 17:26-30). Christ's second coming will be for judgment (Heb. 9:27-28).

Conclusion

Premillennialism is a speculative approach to Bible prophecy that contradicts many plain statements of Scripture. It needs to be rejected. In the lessons that follow, we will study several of the fundamental concepts of premillennialism, including the rapture, tribulation, Armageddon, and the thousand year reign of Christ on earth.

NOTES

Questions

1. Explain the following concepts:
   a. Postmillennialism: ______
   b. Premillennialism: ______
   c. Amillennialism: ______
2. What does premillennialism believe about the nature of the Lord's kingdom? ______
3. What kind of kingdom did Jesus establish (John 18:36-37)? ______
4. What is the Lord's kingdom (Matt. 16:16-18)? ______
5. Why are men unable to thwart God's purposes (Ps. 2)? ______
6. How does one get into the Lord's kingdom (John 3:3-5)? ______
7. What authority does Jesus presently possess (Matt. 28:18-20)? ______
8. What is presently subject to Christ (Eph. 1:18-21)? ______
9. What position does Jesus presently hold (Acts 2:36; 1 Tim. 6:15)? ______
10. What explanation does premillennialism demand for why Jesus died on the cross? ______
11. When did God plan Jesus' crucifixion (Rev. 13:8)? ______
12. What impact does preaching that Jesus' second coming is near have on one's faith when that coming does not occur for years? ______
13. Who knows when Jesus will come again (Matt. 24:36)? ______
14. How does the "last day" show that the establishment of a 1000-year-reign is impossible (John 6:39-40;11:24)? ______

Lesson 15

What Does the Bible Say About the Rapture?

Our denominational friends sometimes speak of the "rapture." What do our friends mean when they speak of the "rapture" and, more importantly, what does the Bible say about the "rapture"?

The answer to this last question is simple. Get out your concordance and look up the word "rapture." There is no entry for the word. Hence, the Bible says nothing about the "rapture." If men would abide by the rule, "speak where the Bible speaks and be silent where the Bible is silent," there would be no preaching about the rapture. If men would call Bible things by Bible names, questions such as this would not occur.

The rapture is part of premillennial theory and has been widely taught in this society. Car bumper stickers say, "In case of Rapture, this car will be unmanned." A popular gospel song is entitled "I'll See You in the Rapture." Hence, we need to study the "rapture" for the same reason that we need to study "reincarnation" and other popular notions men have about the end times, to understand their beliefs and to learn how to answer them.

What Is the Doctrine of the "Rapture"?

In order to understand what denominational folks mean by the "rapture," let us read what they have written in their own explanations of the doctrine. Salem Kirban wrote,

> Rapture: this refers to the time, prior to the start of the 7 year Tribulation Period, when believing Christians (both dead and alive) will "in the twinkling of an eye" rise up to meet Christ in the air (*Guide to Survival*, 12).

The writer continues: "Sometime in the near future ... several MILLION people will suddenly disappear from this earth ... 'in the twinkling of an eye' (1 Corinthians 15:22)" (22).

The doctrine of the "rapture" is part of the warp and woof of premillennial speculation. The rapture is expected to be that occasion at a secret coming of the Lord in which he will remove his saints from this earth before the period of "tribulation." See chart at the bottom of the page.

The Speculation about the Rapture Contradicts the Bible

Premillennial speculation about the end times is a package. One cannot accept one portion of the doctrine without accepting other aspects of it. What was said about the theory of premillennialism in Lesson 14 applies to every aspect of the doctrine, including its speculation about the rapture, Armageddon, the Tribulation,

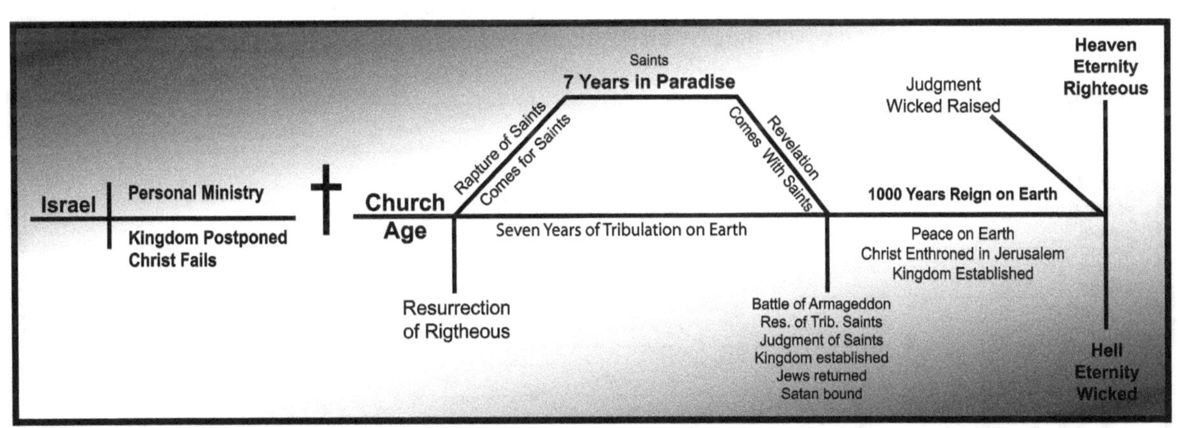

and the thousand year reign of Christ. Here are some things that the rapture speculation does to Bible doctrine.

1. The doctrine teaches several resurrections from the dead. According the premillennialism, there will be a resurrection of the righteous dead at the time of the rapture and a resurrection of the wicked dead at the day of judgment 1007 years later. But the Scriptures speak of one resurrection (John 5:28-29; Acts 24:15).

The events of the "last day" are these: (a) Resurrection will occur (John 11:24); (b) Believers will be raised on the last day (John 6:39, 40); (c) Judgment will occur on that day (John 12:48).

2. The doctrine teaches several comings of the Lord. According to premillennialism, there will be a "quiet" (or secret) coming of the Lord when he snatches away his saints, another coming with his saints to establish his kingdom on earth and reign for 1000 years, and a final coming in judgment. The Scriptures do not speak of a secret coming of the Lord. Rather, it speaks of a time when Jesus will be seen like lightning from one end of heaven to the other (Matt. 24:26-27). Every eye shall see him when he comes (Rev. 1:7). Instead of being a silent, secret coming, Peter said this about the day of the Lord, "But the day of the Lord will come as a thief in the night; in the which the heavens shall pass away with a great noise, and the elements shall melt with fervent heat, the earth also and the works that are therein shall be burned up" (2 Pet. 3:10).

3. The doctrine demands that saints who have made it to heaven must return to this earth for 1000 years. The doctrine that saints will be brought back from heaven to occupy the earth for 1000 years is full of all kinds of problems. Can these saints be guilty of sin during the 1000 years? If so, can they fall from the salvation which they received as a reward for their faithfulness during their earth life? When I make it to heaven, I will not voluntarily leave there to come back to this earth!

4. The doctrine demands the rebuilding of the Temple in Jerusalem. The premillennial concept of the end times expects the Jews to rebuild the Temple in Jerusalem. The rebuilding of the Temple will result in the re-institution of animal sacrifices. The popular premillennial writer Hal Lindsey wrote, "There remains but one more event to completely set the stage for Israel's part in the last great act of her historical drama. This is to rebuild the ancient Temple of worship upon its old site" (*The Late Great Planet Earth,* 45). He continued, "The Israelis will then be permitted to re-institute the sacrifice and offering aspect of the law of Moses. This demands that the Temple be rebuilt, because according to the Law of Moses, sacrifices can be offered only in the Temple at Jerusalem" (140).

What reason is there for the re-institution of animal sacrifices? The Lord brought an end to these sacrifices because the blood of Christ is the all-sufficient atonement for sin. Why would anyone want them re-instated? Premillennial doctrine undermines the all-sufficiency of the blood of Jesus to atone for sin.

5. The doctrine of the rapture is part of an eschatalogical system which has these consequences:

- Makes Jesus a failure (John 18:37).
- Dethrones Christ (Matt. 28:18; 1 Tim. 6:15).
- Breaks the promises of God (Ps. 2; Isa. 53:3). The Lord promised to establish his kingdom despite men's efforts to stop it.
- Convicts the apostles as being false interpreters of Bible prophecy (cf. Acts 13:33; Ps. 2; 132:11; Acts 2:30-33).

NOTES

- Removes Christ's priesthood (Heb. 4:14; 7:17; Zech. 6:12-13). Jesus is to be priest on his throne; if his throne is not yet established neither is his priesthood.
- Denies that the last days began on Pentecost (Acts 2:16-21).
- Changes the nature of the Lord's kingdom to a physical kingdom (John 18:37).
- Blends Christianity with Judaism by its hope of the rebuilding of the Temple.

A Study of 1 Thessalonians 4:13-18, the Passage Used to Teach the Rapture

The premillennialists teach that the dead saints and living saints will be removed from this earth at a secret, quiet coming of Jesus. This passage does not speak of a a quiet coming. The text says that Jesus will come "with a shout, with the voice of the archangel, and with the trump of God" (1 Thess. 4:16). Furthermore, this text does not speak of two comings of Jesus separated by seven years of tribulation. The distinction in this text is between the living and the dead when Jesus comes back, not between the righteous living and dead and the wicked living and dead!

The context of 1 Thessalonians 4:13-5:4 shows the following:

- The day of Christ's coming is a day when both the righteous and wicked will be raised (5:1-3).
- It will occur without warning like a thief in the night (5:2).
- When Jesus comes to give his saints rest as described in 1 Thessalonians 4:13-18, he will also punish the wicked (2 Thess. 1:7-9). Paul also spoke of the Lord's coming when he told the saints that they would receive "rest when the Lord Jesus shall be revealed from heaven." This rest will come "when the Lord Jesus comes ... in flaming fire taking vengeance on them which know not God." When the saints receive rest, the Lord Jesus shall also dispense "everlasting destruction."
- When Jesus comes in glory, *every* man shall be rewarded according to his works (Matt. 16:27).
- When Jesus comes, every eye (not just the righteous) shall see him (Rev. 1:7).
- The resurrection of the dead, both righteous and wicked, shall occur within an "hour" (John 5:28-29).
- "So shall we ever be with the Lord" cannot be reduced to seven years during which the tribulation occurs on earth (1 Thess. 4:18). At that time, the rest will end and the saints will come back to this earth to live and reign with Jesus for 1000 years, according to premillennialism.

Conclusion

Belief in the rapture is not some harmless doctrine which men have devised. It is part of an eschatology which takes men's eyes off the "one hope" and replaces it with a dream of a 1000 year reign of Christ on earth.

NOTES

Questions

1. What is the premillennial belief known as the "rapture"? ______

2. Describe the premillennial expectation of two resurrections:

   a. ______

   b. ______

3. How much time will transpire between the resurrection of the righteous and the wicked (John 5:28-29; Acts 24:15)? ______

4. What events will transpire on the last day (John 11:24; 6:39-40; 12:48)? ______

5. Name the comings of Christ that premillennialism expects? ______

6. What is said about the second coming that shows it will not be secret (Matt. 24:26-27; Rev. 1:7; 2 Pet. 3:10)? ______

7. What expectation do premillennialists have about the Temple in Jerusalem? ______

8. What does the re-institution of animal sacrifices say about the blood of Jesus? ______

9. How are the following things true about premillennialism:

   a. It makes Jesus a failure (John 18:37)? ______

   b. It dethrones Christ (1 Tim. 6:15)? ______

   c. It breaks God's promises (Psa. 2)? ______

____

d. It convicts the apostles as false witnesses (Acts 13:33; Psa. 2)? ____________________

____

10. What two groups are distinguished in 1 Thessalonians 4:13-18? ____________________

____

11. What things in the text show that the second coming will not be secret? ____________________

____

12. What will happen to the wicked when Jesus comes to give rest to his saints (2 Thess. 1:7-9)? _____

____

13. How many people will be rewarded according to their works when Jesus comes (Matt. 16:27)? ____

____

14. Who will see Jesus when he comes (Rev. 1:7)? ____________________

15. How long will the saints who are taken to be with the Lord going to stay with him (1 Thess. 4:18)?

____

Lesson 16

What Does the Bible Say About the Battle of Armageddon?

The word "Armageddon" appears only one time in the King James Version, in Revelation 16:16. It describes a great and decisive battle in which the forces of the Lord are victorious over his enemies. As much as some denominational preachers speak on the subject, one would think that Armageddon occurs in many different Bible verses and contexts.

With the popularity of premillennialism, the general public is acquainted with certain terms that fit the sequence of events of dispensationalism. For example, such terms as "Rapture," "Battle of Armageddon," "Tribulation," etc. are frequently referred to by those with whom we work. Consequently, people are asking, "What is the Rapture?" "What is the Tribulation?" "What is the Battle of Armageddon?" In this lesson, we will study "the Battle of Armageddon."

The Battle of Armageddon According to Premillennialists

The place that the Battle of Armageddon holds in the sequence of events that premillennialists believe will occur is this. At the end of the "church age," Jesus will come again and take his saints from the earth in what is known as the "rapture." The rest of the people on this earth will continue life as it is at the present.

This will be followed by a seven-year period of tribulation. This period is designed to prepare the nation of Israel for her Messiah. A remnant of the Jews will spread the gospel of Christ to Israel and to some Gentiles who will turn to God. The 144,000 of Revelation are said to be 144,000 men like Billy Graham who will lead men to Christ during this period. The personal Anti-christ will arise to make war against these believers. The Tribulation period will be concluded by the great Battle of Armageddon. The Battle of Armageddon will end when Christ appears and destroys his enemies. Then will begin his thousand-year reign from Jerusalem. See chart below.

In the Battle of Armageddon, that the premillennialists believe will occur, four world powers will enter the conflict. They are (a) Europe. Europe is supposed to have become the United States of Europe by this time. Europe will be under one personal leader who is the Anti-christ. United Europe is understood to be the Roman Empire of the prophecies of Daniel (2:44; 7:7-8). (b) The Russian Confederacy. Russia is identified as "Gog, of the land of Magog, the chief prince of Meshech and Tubal" (Ezek. 38:1-3). Her allies will be Persia, Cush, Put, Gomer, and Togarmah (Ezek. 38:6, 9, 15, 22: 39:4) which are identified as Iraq, Iran, Ethiopia, North Africa, Germany,

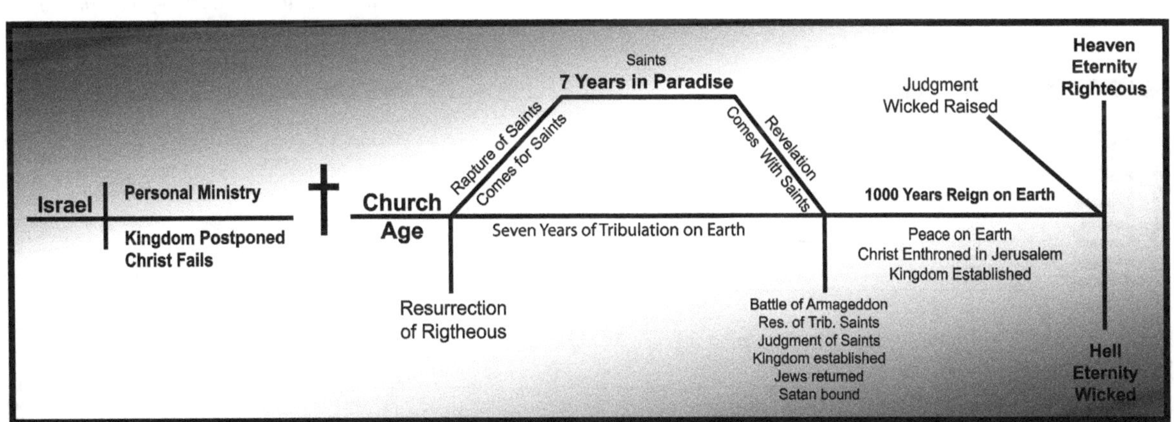

Armenia, etc. (c) King of the South: Egypt. The battle of Armageddon is supposed to be described in Daniel 11. Verse 40 speaks of the "king of the south" which is understood to be Egypt. (d) East. The fourth great power will be a great Eastern power (Dan. 11:44). This is generally understood to be China. (During World War II, premillennialists were thoroughly convinced that it was Japan.)

Here is how the battle will be fought. Egypt will initiate the great conflict against Israel. Because of tensions in the Middle East, premillennialists are convinced that this could happen at any time. At the same time, Russia will invade the Near East pushing its conquests to overrun Egypt and other Arab countries. This could be motivated by Russia's need for oil. Having overrun these countries, Russia will hear of rumors from the East (China) and from the North (Europe under the Anti-christ) and return to Israel (the area around Megiddo) for the onslaught. Through some nuclear holocaust, Russia will be destroyed leaving a "power vacuum" in the Middle East. Europe under the Anti-christ will engage in battle with the East at Armageddon. This will be the last great war. At this point Christ will return to inaugurate his reign of peace in Jerusalem.

Premillennialists have always seen the Battle of Armageddon as imminent. For example, in 1924 William Edward Biederwolf wrote, "In keeping with the interpretation which makes the word descriptive of a characteristic (great slaughter) rather than a definite place, there are those who think the last world war just closed (World War I—mw), was indeed the very battle of Har-Magedon, and that therefore, as John Robertson says, 'The Second Advent of our Lord is now by Prophetical schedule due, and may at the next tick of the watch in your pocket be seen in the sky'" (*The Millennium Bible*, 662-663).

The Battle of Armageddon and Literal Interpretation of Prophecy

The heart of the problem between amillennialists and premillennialists is the hermeneutical problem of whether to interpret prophecies literally, figuratively, or spiritually. Oswald T. Allis said, "One of the most marked features of Premillennialism in all its forms is the emphasis which it places on the literal interpretation of Scripture. It is the insistent claim of its advocates that only when interpreted literally is the Bible interpreted truly; and they denounce as 'spiritualizers' or 'allegorizers' those who do not interpret the Bible with the same degree of literalness as they do. None have made this charge more pointedly than the Dispensationalists. The question of literal versus figurative interpretation is, therefore, one which has to be faced at the very outset" (*Prophecy and the Church,* 16-17).

Premillennialists insist that the biblical prophecies must be interpreted literally. Salem Kirban wrote, "Remember this also: The prophecy that has been fulfilled, *has been fulfilled literally*. More than half of the predictive prophecies concerning Christ, are as yet unfulfilled. As the fulfilled prophecies were fulfilled *literally* ... so the unfulfilled prophecies *will be fulfilled literally*!" (*Guide to Survival*, 14). Hal Lindsey added, "These men used what may be called the golden rule of interpretation which the biblical record of fulfilled prophecy indicates is correct:

> When the plain sense of Scripture makes common sense, seek no other sense; therefore, take every word at its primary, ordinary, usual, literal meaning unless the facts of the immediate context, studied in the light of related passages and axiomatic and fundamental truths, indicate clearly otherwise.
>
> This is the method which this writer has diligently sought to follow" (*The Late Great Planet Earth,* 40).

NOTES

The Premillennialists' insistence that prophecy be interpreted literally leads them to make a number of blunders with the Scriptures.

Though premillennialists affirm the literal interpretation of prophecy, they are inconsistent in their application. There are figures of speech in the Bible that cannot be interpreted literally such as the following: (a) John 10:9—was Jesus literally a door? (b) 1 Corinthians 11:24-25—were the bread and fruit of the vine literally Christ's body and blood? (c) Isaiah 40:3-5—This is expressly said to be fulfilled in the ministry of John the Baptist (Luke 3:4-6). Was it literally fulfilled? Was there anything in the context of Isaiah to indicate that it would not be literally fulfilled? (d) Ezekiel 37:24-26—This passage is interpreted by premillennialists as a Messianic prophecy foretelling the restoration of Israel to the land of Canaan during the millennium. But, if this is going to be given a strict literal interpretation, then David will be the king of Israel at that time. He will have to be raised from the dead and he, not Jesus, will be the king of the millennium.

Premillennialists do not follow their hermeneutical rules consistently. For example, consider Revelation 9:17. "And thus I saw the horses in the vision, and them that sat on them, having breastplates of fire, and of jacinth, and brimstone: and the heads of the horses were as the heads of lions; and out of their mouths issued fire and smoke and brimstone." This description of a great battle in the book of Revelation is given far-fetched and less than literal interpretation. Salem Kirban said, "I am today inclined to think that they are a human army with weapons and gas masks. They are either an organized army or a spontaneous army, such as 200 million communists taking to arms suddenly in various parts of Asia . . . Perhaps the army that the world will face is one of a massive invasion of tanks equipped with flame throwers. It may however, be a dispersant of nerve gas or some biological warfare" (Salem Kirban, *Revelation Visualized*, 204, 207)

On the same passage Hal Lindsey wrote, "The thought may have occurred to you that this is strikingly similar to the phenomena associated with thermonuclear warfare. In fact, many Bible expositors believe that this is an accurate first-century description of a twentieth-century thermonuclear war" (*The Late Great Planet Earth* 71).

Otis Gatewood observed, "Mr. Lindsey would have us believe that Ezekiel 37, 38, 39 refer to the invasion of Palestine by Russia in the last times (pp. 59-71). But the literal interpretation of Ezekiel 37, 38, 39 declares that the weapons of Gog and Magog are swords, shields, helmets, horses, bucklers (Ezekiel 38:4), bows, arrows, hand staves, and spears (Ezekiel 39:9). Can't you just see Russia, who is now equipped with all the latest jets, atomic bombs, tanks, etc., returning to the use of swords, hand staves, spears, etc., when they invade Israel? How long would they last, with such weapons, against Israel's modern weaponry?" (*Book Review of The Late Great Planet Earth*, 5).

The insistence on literalism leads to the following problems: (a) Ignoring the plain statement of scripture. God spoke in divers manners (Heb. 1:1-2). Not all that God spoke was intended to be interpreted literally. (2) Ignoring the New Testament interpretation of prophecy. James D. Bales wrote, "The New Testament interpretation of prophecy is the inspired interpretation of prophecy. How foolish one must be who maintains that the light furnished by the fulfillment, as set forth in God's word, is no clearer than the light set forth in the stage of the unfulfilled" (*Prophecy and Premillennialism,*

NOTES

33). A number of passages understood by premillennialists to be fulfilled in the future are said to be already fulfilled by the inspired writers of the New Testament, such as Psalm 2 (see Acts 13:33) and Psalm 132:11(see Acts 2:30-33).

Consequences of Premillennialism

The Battle of Armageddon is not an isolated doctrine. It is part of a doctrinal system known as premillennialism (see Lesson 14). Premillennialism is a system that has several major consequences for Bible doctrine, such as the following:

- It dethrones Christ (Heb. 1:8; 1 Cor. 15:24, 25; Eph. 1:22; James 4:12; Matt. 28:18; 1 Tim. 6:15).
- Makes Jesus a failure. Jesus said that he was born to be a king and that "for this cause came I into the world" (John 18:37). Did he fail?
- Breaks the promises of God. God declared that he knew that the rulers of earth and the people of Israel would take counsel against his anointed (Psa. 2; Isa. 53:3). "Yet have I set my king upon my holy hill of Zion" (Psa. 2:6). Therefore, God foreknew the plot of his enemies and the rejection of Jesus, and promised that despite that Jesus would be king. If Jesus is not now King, God broke his promises.
- Convicts the apostles as being false interpreters of prophecy (Acts 13:33; Psa. 2; 132:11; Acts 2:30-33).
- Removes Christ's priesthood (Heb. 4:14; 7:17). Zechariah 6:12, 13 states that Christ "shall be a priest upon his throne." If his throne is not now, he is not priest now!
- Postpones the last days (cf. Acts 2:16-21; Heb. 1:1-2).
- Provides for days after the last day. The resurrection is to occur in the last day (John 6:44). Yet, premillennialists say that there will be at least 365,000 days after the last day.
- Alters the nature of the kingdom. The kingdom which Jesus established was spiritual (John 18:37; Luke 17:20-21). Premillennialists want to make it an earthly kingdom that is quite physical.
- Confuses Christianity and Judaism. Premillennialists await the rebuilding of the Temple and re-institution of animal sacrifices.
- Nullifies salvation for the Gentiles. James argued that Gentiles could be brought into the kingdom of God because the prophecy of Amos 9:11-12 was fulfilled (Acts 15:14-17). Premillennialists deny that the passage has been fulfilled. Hence, Gentiles cannot be a part of the kingdom of God today.

What Is Armageddon?

There is very little disagreement as to the meaning of this word which appears only in Revelation 16:16. It is derived from the Hebrew *har megiddo* which means "Mount of Megiddo." Megiddo is a city located on the western end of the Valley of Esdraelon. Through this valley passed many trade routes that brought in much tax revenue. Whoever controlled Megiddo controlled northern Israel. Consequently, it was a strategic military site. Solomon fortified the city during his reign (1 Kings 9:51), as did other kings of Israel. Megiddo was the scene of some very important battles during the Old Testament era. Deborah and Barek defeated Sisera and his host here (Judg. 5:19). Saul and Jonathan fell here against the Philistines (1 Sam. 31:1-3). Pharoah-Necho killed Josiah here (2 Kgs. 23:29; 2 Chron. 35:22). There was a particular appropriateness in the choice of

NOTES

Armageddon as the scene of the last great conflict. Its significance is, therefore, more symbolical than literal. It is designed to show the importance of this battle. Armageddon may very well be used symbolically for a great battlefield rather than a geographical location.

The Battle of Armageddon in the Book of Revelation

The book of Revelation was written by John who was exiled on the Isle of Patmos. It was written to the saints in the seven churches of Asia and concerned itself with things shortly to come to pass (Rev. 1:3). The saints in John's day were undergoing a horrible persecution. The Roman Emperor, in an effort to unify the Empire, demanded that every loyal citizen confess that he was "lord." The emperor was considered "divine." Domitian, the Roman ruler when Revelation was written, delighted in being looked upon as divine and in being so worshiped. To the Christian, such homage was idolatry and an utter denial of faith in Christ. To the Romans, the refusal to worship the emperor was a sign of disloyalty to the State and an act of treason. Emperor worship was forced upon the Christians as a test of loyalty to the State. To refuse to worship the Emperor was treason; to worship the Emperor was a denial of Christianity. Those who refused to worship the Emperor were persecuted. A sharp conflict was inevitable. The forms of punishment used by the Roman government were many. Some were put to death, some were exiled, some were tortured into a confession of the divinity of the emperor, some had their property confiscated, and some received combinations of these measures.

The book of Revelation is designed to reassure the Christian that these persecutions could not destroy Christianity from the face of the earth or keep the Christian from winning the ultimate victory through Jesus Christ. Hence, in symbolical language, John described the great conflict which was occurring between Christ and Satan. The battle is described using these figures: (a) A great red dragon: Satan (12:3); (b) The first beast: the government of the Roman Empire (13:1-10); (c) The second beast: false religion (13:11-18), specifically the emperor worship; (d) Babylon the Great, the great Harlot: Rome.

In the recorded conflict, Satan gathered all of his forces together against God (16:12-16). The conflict occurred and God was victorious. The great city of Babylon the Great was decimated (16:17-18:24). The beast and the false prophet were destroyed (19:17-21). The Great Dragon was defeated (20:7-10). The victory belongs to Christ and his saints (cf. 19:7-16). Hence, the Battle of Armageddon is the employment of symbolical language to tell the persecuted saints that God would ultimately be victorious over Satan. The language could be easily understood by saints acquainted with the symbols of the Old Testament but was mysterious to non-Christians.

Conclusion

The Battle of Armageddon does not describe some literal battle between Russia, Egypt, Europe, and China. That would have had absolutely no meaning to first-century Christians. The Premillennial concept of the Battle of Armageddon is part and parcel of a system of infidelity. Rather, the Battle of Armageddon was a symbolical method of revealing God's ultimate victory over Satan.

NOTES

Questions

1. What is the Battle of Armageddon according to premillennialism? __________

2. When will it be fought? __________

3. What four nations will fight in the Battle of Armageddon? __________

4. What have premillennialists said about when the Battle of Armageddon will occur through the years?

5. What is the primary difference between premillennialists and amillennialists on the interpretation of prophecy? __________

6. Why can't the Bible always be interpreted literally? __________

7. Cite three examples to demonstrate that literal interpretation cannot always be given to every Bible verse. (See if you can find one example other than those cited in this book.) __________

8. Give your impression of the premillennial interpretation of Revelation 9:17 as cited in this lesson (see paragraphs 3-4, p. 105). __________

9. List four consequences of premillennialism:

   a. __________

   b. __________

   c. __________

   d. __________

10. What does "Armageddon" mean? __________

11. Why was Megiddo important? __________

12. Give the meaning of the Battle of Armageddon in Revelation. __________

Lesson 17

What Does the Bible Say about the 1000 Year Reign of Christ?

Many Christians believe that Jesus is going to return to this earth one day and establish an earthly kingdom in Jerusalem over which he will rule for 1000 years. This doctrine is part of an eschatological system known as premillennialism or dispensationalism. Bernard Ramm wrote, "Premillennialiam is the belief that Christ will return and set up a glorious earthly kingdom which will last a thousand years. This kingdom is the interim period between the return of Christ and the final judgment. It differs from amillennialism which sees the reign of Christ in the Church and therefore not demanding a visible reign" (*A Handbook of Contemporary Theology,* 83). The belief in a thousand year reign of Christ on earth is part of a theological system based on a misinterpretation of God's work in Christ.

Revelation 20

The book of Revelation has been given various speculative interpretations as commentators try to fit its teaching into preconceived ideas of what will occur in the end times. Particularly has Revelation 20 been wrested to fit into many schemes. Benjamin Warfield observed, "Nothing, indeed, seems to have been more common in all ages of the Church than to frame an eschatological scheme from this passage, imperfectly understood, and then to impose this scheme on the rest of Scripture" (*Biblical Doctrines,* 643).

The premillennial interpretation of Revelation states that Christ will come back in his second coming to this earth and reign for a literal 1000 years in the city of Jerusalem over all of the earth. The essential details of the premillennial speculation are not found in Revelation 20, such as the following:

- Jerusalem
- The second coming of Christ
- A reign on earth
- A bodily resurrection
- "Us." Rather, this passage applies to martyred saints
- Christ on earth
- A literal throne

When premillennialists are pressed on their interpretation of Revelation, they insist that the 1000 years of Revelation be interpreted literally. Why should that be interpreted literally when so many other things in the chapter are obviously used in a figurative sense? Here are some figurative things in Revelation 19-20:

- A white horse and rider (19:11)
- Heavenly armies with horses going to war (19:14-15)
- Sword out of Jesus' mouth (19:15)
- Jesus having eyes that are a flame of fire (19:12)
- Jesus ruling with a rod of iron (19:15)
- Jesus treads the winepress (19:15)
- Birds eating bodies of those slain (19:17-18)
- The Beast (19:19)
- Mark of beast (19:20)
- Abyss or bottomless pit (20:1)
- Key to pit (20:1)
- Chain (20:1)
- 1000 years (20:2)
- First resurrection (20:5)
- Second death (20:6)

To make the 1000 year reign a literal thousand years of earthly reign would be to take a highly figurative text and arbitrarily literalize what one wishes from the passage. If one is going to literally interpret the 1000 years, he is logically compelled to make everything else literal.

What Is the 1000 Year Reign of Christ?

The following two quotations explain what the 1000 year reign of Christ is.

R.C.H. Lenski: "The 1,000 years cover the whole period from 12:2 to 20:6, from the appearance of Satan as the dragon (12:3) to his final judgment (20:7-10).... These 1,000 years thus extend from the incarnation and the enthronement of the Son (12:5) to Satan's final plunge into hell (20:10), which is the entire New Testament period" (*The Interpretation of St. John's Revelation*, 564-565).

Anthony Hoekema: "The period, as we saw, spans the entire New Testament dispensation, from the time of the first coming of Christ to just before the Christ's second coming" (Anthony Hoekema, *The Bible and the Future*, 230).

In a word, *the 1000 year reign of Christ is a symbolical description of his present reign, covering the period of time from his ascension into heaven until the second coming.* We presently are living in the reign of Christ, as is indicated by such clear statements of Jesus' present reign as Matthew 28:18; Acts 2:36; Ephesians 1:20-23; and 1 Timothy 6:15.

What Happens to Those Who Die in Christ?

Revelation 20 should be interpreted to harmonize with what the rest of Revelation says. Revelation 20 portrays those martyred saints who were living and reigning with Christ for a 1000 years. What the rest of Revelation says about the dead saints is consistent with Revelation 20. Consider these texts:

> To him that overcometh will I grant to sit with me in my throne, even as I also overcame, and am set down with my Father in his throne (Rev. 3:21).
>
> And when he had opened the fifth seal, I saw under the altar the souls of them that were slain for the word of God, and for the testimony which they held: And they cried with a loud voice, saying, How long, O Lord, holy and true, dost thou not judge and avenge our blood on them that dwell on the earth? And white robes were given unto every one of them; and it was said unto them, that they should rest yet for a little season, until their fellowservants also and their brethren, that should be killed as they were, should be fulfilled (Rev. 6:9-11).
>
> After this I beheld, and, lo, a great multitude, which no man could number, of all nations, and kindreds, and people, and tongues, stood before the throne, and before the Lamb, clothed with white robes, and palms in their hands; and cried with a loud voice, saying, Salvation to our God which sitteth upon the throne, and unto the Lamb (Rev. 7:9-10).
>
> And one of the elders answered, saying unto me, What are these which are arrayed in white robes? And whence came they? And I said unto him, Sir, thou knowest. And he said to me, These are they which came out of great tribulation, and have washed their robes, and made them white in the blood of the Lamb (Rev. 7:13-14).
>
> And I looked, and, lo, a Lamb stood on the mount Sion, and with him an hundred forty and four thousand, having his Father's name written in their foreheads. And I heard a voice from heaven, as the voice of many waters, and as the voice of a great thunder: and I heard the voice of harpers harping with their harps: and they sung as it were a new song before the throne, and before the four beasts, and the elders: and no man could learn that song but the hundred and forty and four thousand, which were redeemed from the earth (Rev. 14:1-3).
>
> And I heard a voice from heaven saying unto me, Write, Blessed are the dead which die in the Lord from henceforth: Yea, saith the Spirit, that they may rest from their labours; and their works do follow them (Rev. 14:13).

The picture presented in Revelation of the martyred saints living and reigning with Christ for a 1000 years describes those saints whose bodies are dead, but who are alive in the spirit, during the time between their death and the Lord's second coming.

The condition of the departed saints should be carefully observed (20:4). The saints had died,

NOTES

giving their life for the word of God (20:4). These dead saints are pictured as "reigning with Christ" (see Rev. 3:21). Those deceased believers had come to life and were reigning with Christ (cf. 6:9-11). Their coming to life was described as the "first resurrection" to distinguish it from the resurrection at the end of time (Rev. 20:11-13). What John sees is that the dead saints have not perished; they are alive and well, reigning with Christ in heaven during the intermediate time between their death and his second coming (cf. Phil. 1:23; 2 Cor. 5:8; also Luke 20:37-38).

They reigned for 1000 years (20:4). The 1000 years is used to describe the present reign of Christ in heaven. The figure 1000 is not literal; it is used figuratively to refer to the completeness of Christ's reign.

The "rest of the dead" did not live and reign with Christ (20:5). The "rest of the dead" refers to the "unbelievers" who died. Their not living and reigning with Christ is a description of their being out of Christ's fellowship. The phrase "until the 1000 years are ended" does not imply that they then entered into Christ's reign at the end of the 1000 years, for there is no phrase that follows which so states. The second death that has no power over the believing dead has power over the unbelieving dead (20:6).

What Is the Binding of Satan (20:1-3)?

The time period of the binding of Satan is between the Lord's first and second coming, during the gospel dispensation. The activity of Satan described in Revelation is his war against the saints (12:2,17). The threat to the saints was that through Satan's persecution the church would be destroyed. The binding of Satan indicates that the Lord will restrain his activity so that he does not destroy the church.

The gospels speak of the binding of Satan. Jesus used the illustration of binding the strong man and looting his house to describe what happened when he cast out demons (Matt. 12:29). The apostles' work manifested the restraining of the devil (Luke 10:17-18). The victory of Christ through the cross was the casting out of Satan (John 12:31-32).

The loosing of Satan to deceive the nations shortly before the second coming may refer to an intense period of suffering and persecution shortly before the Lord's second coming (20:7-8). Gog and Magog "symbolized all the heathen enemies of God's people from the time of the prophets to the Roman Empire, all who sought to thwart His purpose and to destroy the church" (Hailey, 397). These will bring their forces against the Lord's people but will be destroyed by the Lord (20:9-10).

What We Can Expect for the Future: The Second Coming of Christ

His coming will be an unexpected coming, like a thief in the night (2 Pet. 3:10). At that time, the earth will be destroyed (2 Pet. 3:10). All will be raised from the dead (John 5:28-29; Rev. 20:11-15). The day of grace has ended (Matt. 25:6-10). Judgment will immediately follow (Rev. 20:11-15). There is no space for a literal 1000 year reign of Christ on this earth.

Conclusion

The 1000 year reign of Christ does not refer to Jesus coming to this earth and establishing an earthly kingdom over which he will reign for a thousand years. Rather, it refers to his present reign in heaven and to his saints who have passed on reigning with him.

NOTES

Questions

1. Define "premillennialism." ______________________________

____

2. What do premillennialists expect to occur when Jesus comes back again? ______________________________

____

3. List five things necessary to the premillennial expectation of a literal 1000 year reign that are not found in Revelation 20:

   a. ______________________________

   b. ______________________________

   c. ______________________________

   d. ______________________________

   e. ______________________________

4. Give seven things in Revelation 19:11-20:7 that indicate that the passage should be interpreted figuratively:

   a. ______________________________

   b. ______________________________

   c. ______________________________

   d. ______________________________

   e. ______________________________

   f. ______________________________

   g. ______________________________

5. What mistake in the rules of interpretation do premillennialists make when explaining Revelation 20?

____

6. What is the 1000 year reign of Christ? ______________________________

____

7. How do the following passages prove that Christ is presently reigning:

   a. Matthew 28:18? ______________________________

   b. Acts 2:36? ______________________________

   c. Ephesians 1:20-23? ______________________________

d. 1 Timothy 6:15? ______

8. Whom did John see alive under the altar (Rev. 20:4)? ______

______

9. What happens to the righteous dead according to the book of Revelation (3:21; 6:9-11; 7:9-10, 13-14; 14:1-3, 13)? ______

______

10. If the 1000 years used in Revelation is figurative, what does it mean? ______

______

11. When did the binding of Satan occur (20:1-2)? ______

______

12. What does the binding of Satan mean? ______

______

www.ingramcontent.com/pod-product-compliance
Lightning Source LLC
LaVergne TN
LVHW081252100826
845148LV00009B/1204
* 9 7 8 1 5 8 4 2 7 0 0 5 8 *